D0886595

Word List of Gregg

THE GREGG PUBLISHING COMPANY

Shorthand Simplified

A DICTIONARY OF 30,000 AUTHORITATIVE
GREGG SHORTHAND OUTLINES

John Robert Gregg

Louis A. Leslie

Charles E. Zoubek

Business Education Division, McGraw-Hill Book Company, Inc.

New York   Chicago   San Francisco   Dallas   Toronto   London

WORD LIST OF GREGG SHORTHAND SIMPLIFIED

Copyright, 1949, by The Gregg Publishing Company. Copyrighted in the United States of America, Great Britain and Ireland, France, Italy, and Spain. All rights reserved. This book, or parts thereof, may not be reproduced in any form without permission of the publishers.

Sept. 1949-NP-100

Shorthand Plates Written by

CHARLES RADER

PUBLISHED BY THE GREGG PUBLISHING COMPANY

Business Education Division of the McGraw-Hill Book Company, Inc.

Printed in the United States of America

FOREWORD

Word List of Gregg Shorthand Simplified is a shorthand dictionary divided into three parts:

Part One contains, in alphabetic order, the shorthand outlines for 26,098 words. These 26,098 words, however, represent a considerably larger vocabulary, as many simple derivatives—those ending in *-ing* and *-s*, for example, which present no stenographic problem—have been omitted.

Part Two contains, in alphabetic order, the shorthand outlines for 2,604 entries for personal and geographical names.

Part Three consists of a list of 72 shorthand outlines for abbreviations such as *f.o.b.* and *C.O.D.*

It is easily possible to construct briefer outlines for many of the scientific and literary words for which full outlines are given in this dictionary. It is not advisable to do so, however, unless the writer is certain that he will use those briefer outlines with sufficient frequency to justify the effort of learning them. Otherwise, the brief but half-remembered outline will cause mental hesitation that will result in slower rather than faster writing.

The experience of expert shorthand writers of every system is conclusive in establishing the inadvisability of attempting to gain speed by devising and learning lists of brief outlines. Longer outlines that are quickly constructed by the mind under pressure of dictation give the writer more speed; the attempt to remember and use large numbers of abbreviated outlines tends to reduce the writer's speed.

It is hoped that this volume will render a useful service to the shorthand writer by placing at his disposal a facile and fluent outline for any word in which he may be interested.

The Publishers

PART ONE

Part One of this *Word List* contains 26,098 word entries alphabetically arranged.

Experience has proved that those using a shorthand dictionary often consult it for the simple words formerly omitted from shorthand dictionaries or for rare and unusual words likewise formerly omitted.

The present list, therefore, includes many of the apparently simple words formerly omitted. It includes many of the simple derivatives formerly omitted. Most readily apparent will be the addition of the many rare and unusual words that experience has proved are wanted by users of such a list as this.

Many words are included because the shorthand learner, while still in school, has occasion to use them in his schoolwork. For this reason, many mathematical, mineralogical, chemical, physical, botanical, and physiological terms are included. For the same reason, many literary words are included, words that are of no business value but that the high school or college learner uses in schoolwork. The bulk of the vocabulary, however, consists of words used in business-office dictation.

Consistency, rather than brevity of outline, has been the guiding principle in the construction of the shorthand outlines in this *Word List of Gregg Shorthand Simplified*. The fastest shorthand outline (within reasonable limits) is the outline that requires the least mental effort, the outline that is written consistently and analogically. The speed of a short-hand outline is not to be judged by its brevity to the eye, nor even by its facility for the hand; it is to be judged by the speed with which it may be constructed by the mind and supplied by the mind to the hand.

A

abacus
abaft
abalone
abandon
abandoned
abandonment
abase
abasement
abash
abatable
abate
abated
abatement
abbess
abbey
abbot
abbreviate
abbreviated
abbreviation
abdicate
abdicated
abdication
abdomen
abdominal
abduct
abducted
abduction

abed
aberration
abet
abetted
abettor
abeyance
abhor
abhorred
abhorrence
abhorrent
abide
ability
abject
abjuration
abjure
abjured
ablative
ablaze
able
ablest
ablution
ably
abnegation
abnormal
abnormality
abnormity
aboard

abode
abolish
abolition
abolitionist
abominable
abominate
abomination
aboriginal
aborigines
abortive
abound
aboundingly
about
above
abrade
abraded
abrasion
abrasive
abreast
abridge
abridged
abridgment
abroad
abrogate
abrogated
abrogation
abrupt

1

abscess	abstract	accelerate
abscissa	abstracted	accelerated
abscond	abstractedly	acceleration
absconded	abstraction	accelerative
absconder	abstractly	accelerator
absence	abstruse	accent
absent	absurd	accented
absentee	absurdity	accentuate
absently	absurdly	accentuation
absinth	abundance	accept
absolute	abundant	acceptability
absolutely	abuse	acceptable
absolution	abused	acceptance
absolutism	abusive	acceptation
absolutist	abusively	access
absolve	abusiveness	accessibility
absorb	abut	accessible
absorbed	abutment	accession
absorbent	abutter	accessory
absorbingly	abysm	accidence
absorption	abysmal	accident
absorptive	abyss	accidental
abstain	acacia	accidentally
abstained	academic	accipitrine
abstainer	academician	acclaim
abstemious	academies	acclaimed
abstemiously	academy	acclamation
abstemiousness	Acadian	acclamatory
abstention	acanthus	acclimate
abstinence	accede	acclimated
abstinent	acceded	acclimation

2

acclimatization
acclimatize
acclimatized
acclivity
accolade
accommodate
accommodated
accommodatingly
accommodation
accommodative
accompaniment
accompanist
accompany
accomplice
accomplish
accomplished
accomplishment
accord
accordance
accorded
accordingly
accordion
accost
accosted
account
accountability
accountable
accountancy
accountant
accounted
accoutered

accouterment
accredit
accredited
accretion
accrual
accrue
accrued
accumulate
accumulated
accumulates
accumulation
accumulative
accumulator
accuracy
accurate
accurately
accusation
accusative
accuse
accused
accuser
accustom
accustomed
ace
acerb
acerbity
acetate
acetic
acetone
acetylene
ache

achieve
achieved
achievement
achromatic
achromatosis
acid
acidification
acidify
acidity
acidly
acidosis
acidulate
acidulous
acknowledge
acknowledged
acknowledgment
acme
acne
acolyte
aconite
acorn
acoustic
acoustical
acoustics
acquaint
acquaintance
acquaintanceship
acquainted
acquiesce
acquiescence
acquiescent

3

acquire	actor	addicted
acquirement	actress	addiction
acquires	actual	addition
acquisition	actualities	additional
acquisitive	actuality	additionally
acquisitiveness	actually	additive
acquit	actuary	address
acquittal	actuate	addressed
acquitted	actuated	addressee
acre	acuity	addressograph
acreage	acumen	adduce
acrid	acute	adduct
acridity	acutely	adduction
acrimonious	acuteness	adductive
acrimoniously	adage	adductor
acrimony	adagio	adenoid
acrobat	adamant	adenology
acrobatic	adamantine	adenoma
acropolis	adapt	adept
across	adaptability	adequacy
acrostic	adaptable	adequately
act	adaptation	adhere
acted	adapted	adhered
actinic	adapter	adherence
actinium	adaptive	adherent
action	add	adhesion
actionable	added	adhesive
activate	addenda	adieu
active	addendum	adipose
activities	adder	adjacency
activity	addict	adjacent

4

adjective
adjoin
adjoined
adjourn
adjourned
adjournment
adjudge
adjudged
adjudicate
adjudicated
adjudication
adjudicator
adjunct
adjuration
adjuratory
adjure
adjured
adjust
adjustable
adjusted
adjuster
adjustment
adjutancy
adjutant
administer
administered
administration
administrative
administratively
administrator
administratrix

admirable
admirably
admiral
admiralty
admiration
admire
admired
admissibility
admissible
admission
admit
admittance
admitted
admittedly
admixture
admonish
admonished
admonition
admonitory
adobe
adolescence
adolescent
adopt
adopted
adoption
adoptive
adorable
adoration
adore
adored
adoringly

adorn
adorned
adornment
adrenal
adrenaline
adrift
adroit
adroitly
adsorption
adulation
adulatory
adult
adulterant
adulterate
adulterated
adulteration
adulterer
adulterous
adultery
adumbrate
adumbration
advance
advanced
advancement
advantage
advantageous
advent
adventitious
adventure
adventurer
adventuresome

adventuress	aerated	affix
adventurous	aeration	affixed
adverb	aerial	afflatus
adverbial	aerie	afflict
adverbially	aeronautical	afflicted
adversary	affability	affliction
adversative	affable	affluence
adverse	affably	affluent
adversely	affair	afford
adversity	affect	afforded
advert	affectation	affray
advertise	affected	affright
advertised	affectedly	affront
advertisement	affectingly	affronted
advice	affection	afghan
advisability	affectionate	afield
advisable	affectionately	afire
advisably	affiance	aflame
advise	affianced	afloat
advised	affiant	afoot
advisedly	affidavit	aforementioned
advisement	affiliate	aforesaid
advisory	affiliated	aforetime
advocacy	affiliation	afoul
advocate	affinity	afraid
advowson	affirm	afresh
adz	affirmation	after
aegis	affirmative	afterdeck
Aeolian	affirmatory	after-dinner
aeon	affirmed	aftereffect
aerate	affirmingly	afterglow

6

afterlife
aftermath
afternoon
aftertaste
afterthought
afterward
again
against
agape
agate
agateware
agave
age
aged
ageless
agency
agenda
agendum
agent
ageratum
agglomerate
agglomeration
agglomerative
agglutinate
agglutination
agglutinative
aggrandize
aggrandizement
aggravate
aggravated
aggravatingly

aggravation
aggregate
aggregation
aggression
aggressive
aggressor
aggrieved
aghast
agile
agilely
agility
agio
agitate
agitated
agitation
agitator
agnate
agnostic
agnosticism
agonize
agonizingly
agony
agrarian
agree
agreeability
agreeable
agreed
agreement
agricultural
agriculture
agronomy

ague
ahead
ahoy
ahungered
aid
aided
aigrette
aiguillette
ail
ailanthus
ailed
aileron
ailment
aim
aimless
air
aired
airily
airship
airway
airy
aisle
ajar
akimbo
alabaster
alacrity
alamo
alarm
alarmed
alarmingly
alarmist

alas	alimentary	allocation
albatross	alimony	allocution
albino	aliquot	allopath
album	alive	allopathy
albumin	alizarin	allot
albuminous	alkali	allotment
alchemy	alkalinity	allotted
alcohol	all	allow
alcoholic	allay	allowable
alcoholism	allegation	allowance
alcove	allege	alloy
alder	alleged	alloyed
alderman	allegedly	allspice
aldermanic	allegiance	allude
aleatory	allegorical	alluded
alembic	allegory	allure
alert	allergic	allured
alertly	allergy	alluringly
alexandrite	alleviate	allusion
alfalfa	alleviated	allusive
algebra	alleviation	allusively
alias	alley	alluvial
alibi	alleyway	ally
alien	alliance	almanac
alienable	allied	almighty
alienate	alligator	almond
alienation	alliteration	almoner
alienist	alliterative	almost
alight	alliteratively	alms
alignment	allocate	almshouse
alike	allocated	aloe

8

aloft

aloha

alone

along

aloof

aloofly

alopecia

aloud

alpaca

alphabet

alphabetic

alphabetical

alphabetize

already

also

altar

altarpiece

alter

alterable

alteration

alterative

altercation

alternate

alternated

alternation

alternative

alternator

although

altitude

alto

altogether

altruism

altruist

altruistic

alum

aluminate

aluminum

alumni

alumnus

alveolus

always

alyssum

amalgamate

amalgamated

amalgamation

amanuensis

amaranth

amass

amateur

amateurish

amative

amatory

amaze

amazed

amazingly

Amazon

ambassador

ambassadorial

amber

ambidextrous

ambient

ambiguity

ambiguous

ambition

ambitious

ambitiously

amble

ambrosia

ambrosial

ambulance

ambulatory

ambuscade

ambush

ameliorate

ameliorated

ameliorative

amen

amenable

amend

amended

amendment

amends

amenity

American

Americanization

Americanize

amethyst

amiability

amiable

amicable

amidships

amiss

amity

ammonia	amputate	anastigmatic
ammonium	amputated	anathematize
ammunition	amputation	anatomic
amnesia	amuck	anatomical
amnesty	amulet	anatomist
amoeba	amulets	anatomize
among	amuse	anatomy
amongst	amused	ancestor
amorous	amusement	ancestral
amorously	amusingly	ancestry
amorphous	anachronism	anchor
amortization	anachronistic	anchorage
amortize	anachronous	anchored
amortized	anaconda	anchorite
amount	anagram	anchovy
amounted	analects	ancient
amour	analgesia	ancillary
amperage	analgesic	and
ampersand	analogical	andante
amphibian	analogous	andiron
amphibious	analogy	anecdote
amphibiously	analysis	anemia
amphitheater	analyst	anemometer
amphora	analytic	anemone
ample	analytical	anent
amplification	analytically	anesthesia
amplifier	analyze	anesthetic
amplify	anarchical	anesthetize
amplitude	anarchism	angel
amply	anarchist	angelic
ampulla	anarchy	Angelus

10

anger	annihilate	anomaly
angered	annihilated	anon
angle	annihilation	anonymity
angled	anniversary	anonymous
angler	annotate	anopheles
Anglo-Saxon	annotated	another
angrily	annotation	answer
angry	announce	answerable
anguish	announced	answered
angular	announcement	ant
angularity	announcer	antagonism
aniline	annoy	antagonist
animadversion	annoyance	antagonistic
animal	annoyed	antagonize
animate	annoyingly	antagonized
animated	annual	antarctic
animatedly	annually	ante
animation	annuitant	anteater
animator	annuity	antecedent
animosity	annul	antechamber
animus	annular	antedate
anise	annulled	antelope
ankle	annulment	antenatal
anklet	annunciation	antenna
ankylosis	annunciator	anterior
annalist	anode	anteroom
annals	anodyne	anthem
anneal	anoint	anthologist
annealed	anointed	anthology
annex	anomalies	anthracite
annexation	anomalous	anthrax

anthropoid	anxious	apologist
anthropological	any	apologize
anthropology	anybody	apologized
antic	anyhow	apology
anticipate	anyone	apoplectic
anticipated	anything	apoplexy
anticipation	anyway	apostasy
anticipatory	anywhere	apostate
anticlimax	aorta	apostle
antidote	aortic	apostolic
antimony	apart	apostrophe
antinomy	apartment	apostrophize
antipathy	apathetic	apothecary
antiphonal	apathetically	apothegm
antipodes	apathy	apotheosis
antiquarian	aperient	appall
antiquary	aperitive	appalled
antiquated	aperture	appallingly
antique	apex	appanage
antiquity	aphasia	apparatus
antisepsis	aphid	apparel
antiseptic	aphorism	apparent
antithesis	aphoristic	apparition
antithetical	apiary	appeal
antitoxin	apical	appealed
antler	apices	appealingly
antlered	apiece	appear
antonym	apocalypse	appearance
antrum	apogee	appeared
anvil	apologetic	appeasable
anxiety	apological	appease

appeased	applicant	apprenticed
appeasement	application	apprenticeship
appeasingly	applicator	apprise
appellant	applied	apprised
appellate	apply	approach
appellation	appoint	approachable
appellee	appointed	approached
append	appointee	approbation
appendage	appointive	appropriate
appendectomy	appointment	appropriately
appended	apportion	appropriateness
appendicitis	apportioned	appropriation
appendix	apportionment	approval
appendixes	apposite	approve
apperceive	apposition	approved
apperceived	appraisal	approvingly
apperception	appraise	approximate
apperceptive	appraised	approximately
appertain	appraisingly	approximation
appertained	appreciable	appurtenance
appetite	appreciably	appurtenant
appetizer	appreciate	apricot
appetizingly	appreciated	April
applaud	appreciation	apron
applauded	appreciative	apropos
applause	appreciatively	apse
apple	apprehend	apt
applejack	apprehended	aptitude
appliance	apprehension	aptly
applicability	apprehensive	aptness
applicable	apprentice	aquamarine

13

aquarium	archduchess	argumentation
aquatic	archduchy	argumentative
aqueduct	archduke	argyrol
aqueous	archeology	arid
aquiline	archer	aridity
Arab	archery	arise
arabesque	archetype	aristocracy
Arabian	archipelago	aristocrat
Arabic	architect	aristocratic
arable	architectonic	arithmetic
arbiter	architectural	arithmetical
arbitrage	archives	ark
arbitrament	archivist	arm
arbitrarily	archly	armada
arbitrariness	archway	armadillo
arbitrary	arctic	armament
arbitrated	ardent	armature
arbitration	ardently	armchair
arbitrator	ardor	armed
arbor	arduous	Armenian
arboreal	arduously	armful
arboretum	are	armistice
arbutus	area	armlet
arc	arena	armor
arcade	argent	armorial
arcanum	argentiferous	armory
arch	argon	armpit
archaic	Argonaut	armscye
archangel	arguable	army
archbishop	argue	arnica
archdeacon	argument	aroma

14

aromatic	artful	ascribe
arouse	artfully	ascribed
arpeggio	arthritis	ascription
arraign	artichoke	asepsis
arraignment	article	aseptic
arrange	articulate	ash
arranged	articulated	ashamed
arrangement	articulation	ashen
arras	artifact	ashes
array	artifice	ashlar
arrearage	artificial	ashore
arrears	artificiality	ashy
arrest	artificially	Asiatic
arrival	artillery	aside
arrive	artist	asinine
arrogance	artistic	ask
arrogant	artistry	askance
arrogate	artless	askew
arrowhead	Aryan	aslant
arrowy	as	asleep
arroyo	asbestos	asp
arsenal	ascend	asparagus
arsenate	ascendant	aspect
arsenic	ascendency	aspen
arsenical	ascension	asperity
arsenide	ascent	aspersion
arsenite	ascertain	asphalt
arson	ascertainment	asphodel
art	ascetic	asphyxiate
arterial	asceticism	asphyxiation
artery	ascorbic	aspic

15

aspirant	assessor	assumed
aspirate	asset	assumpsit
aspiration	asseverate	assumption
aspire	asseveration	assurance
aspired	assiduity	assure
aspirin	assiduous	assured
assagai	assiduously	assuredly
assailant	assign	Assyrian
assassin	assignable	aster
assassinate	assigned	asterisk
assassinated	assignee	astern
assassination	assignment	asteroid
assault	assignor	asthenia
assaulted	assimilate	asthma
assay	assimilated	asthmatic
assayed	assimilation	astigmatic
assemblage	assist	astigmatism
assemble	assistance	astonish
assembly	assistant	astonishingly
assent	assisted	astonishment
assented	assists	astound
assentingly	associate	astoundingly
assert	associated	astragalus
asserted	association	astrakhan
assertion	associative	astral
assertive	assorted	astray
assertively	assortment	astride
assess	assuage	astringency
assessable	assuaged	astringent
assessed	assumably	astrologer
assessment	assume	astrology

16

astronomer · atonement · attest
astronomical · atrium · attestation
astronomy · atrocious · attests
astute · atrociously · attic
astutely · atrocity · attire
astuteness · atrophied · attired
asunder · atrophy · attitude
asylum · atropine · attitudinize
asymmetric · attach · attorney
asymmetrical · attached · attract
at · attachment · attracted
atavism · attack · attraction
atheism · attacker · attractive
atheist · attain · attractively
atheistic · attainable · attribute
atheneum · attainder · attribution
Athenian · attained · attributive
athlete · attainment · attrition
athletic · attar · auburn
athletics · attempt · auction
athwart · attempted · auctioneer
atmosphere · attend · audacious
atmospheric · attendance · audaciously
atoll · attendant · audacity
atom · attention · audibility
atomic · attentive · audible
atomize · attentively · audibly
atomized · attentiveness · audience
atomizer · attenuate · audit
atone · attenuated · audited
atoned · attenuation · audition

17

auditor	Austrian	availability
auditorium	authentic	available
auditory	authenticate	availed
auger	authentication	avalanche
aught	authenticity	avarice
augment	author	avaricious
augmentation	authoritarian	avariciously
augmentative	authoritative	avatar
augur	authority	avenge
augured	authorization	avenged
augury	authorize	avenue
august	authorized	aver
August	authorship	average
augustly	autobiography	averred
auk	autochthonous	averse
aunt	autocracy	aversion
aura	autocrat	avert
aureole	autocratic	averted
auricle	autograph	aviary
auricular	automatic	aviation
auriferous	automatism	aviator
aurora	automaton	avid
auroral	automobile	avidity
auscultate	autonomous	avidly
auscultation	autonomy	avigation
auspices	autopsy	avocado
auspicious	autosuggestion	avocation
austere	autumn	avoid
austerely	autumnal	avoidable
austerity	auxiliary	avowal
Australian	avail	avowedly

18

avuncular	awash	awoke
await	away	ax
awaited	awestricken	axiom
awake	awestruck	axiomatic
awaken	awful	axis
awakened	awkward	axle
award	awkwardly	azalea
awarded	awkwardness	azimuth
aware	awl	azure
awareness	awning	azurite

B

babbitt	bad	balcony
baboon	badger	bald
baby	badinage	baldachin
baccalaureate	badly	baldric
bacchanal	badminton	bale
bachelor	badness	baled
bachelorhood	baffle	baleful
back	baffled	balk
backboard	bag	ball
backbone	bagged	ballad
backer	bagasse	ballast
backfire	bagatelle	ballerina
backgammon	baggage	ballet
background	bagpipe	ballistics
backhand	bail	balloon
backhanded	bailed	balloonist
backlash	bailiff	ballot
backlog	bailiwick	ballroom
backslide	bailment	balm
backwardness	bait	balsam
backwash	baize	balsamiferous
backwater	bake	baluster
bacon	bakelite	balustrade
bacteria	baker	bamboo
bacterial	bakery	bamboozle
bacteriological	balance	bamboozled
bacteriology	balbriggan	ban

banal	banquet	bareness
banality	banshee	bargain
banana	bantam	bargained
band	banter	barge
bandage	bantered	bargeman
bandanna	banteringly	baritone
bandbox	banyan	barium
bandeau	baptism	bark
banded	baptismal	barley
bandit	Baptist	barn
banditti	baptize	barnacle
bandmaster	baptized	barogram
bandoleer	bar	barograph
bandy	barb	barometer
baneful	barbarian	barometric
bang	barbaric	baron
bangboard	barbarism	baroness
banged	barbarity	baronet
bangle	barbarous	baronetcy
banish	barbecue	baronial
banishment	barbed	baroque
banister	barber	barrack
banjo	barberry	barracuda
bank	barbican	barrage
bankbook	bard	barratry
banked	bare	barrel
banker	bareback	barren
bankrupt	bared	barrenness
bankruptcy	barefaced	barricade
banned	bareheaded	barrier
banner	barely	barrister

21

barrow	bastion	beaker
barter	bat	beam
bartered	batch	beamed
basal	bateau	bean
bascule	bath	bear
base	bather	bearable
baseboard	bathhouse	beard
baseless	bathos	bearded
basely	baton	bearskin
baseman	battalion	beast
basement	batter	beastliness
baseness	battered	beastly
baser	battery	beat
basest	battle	beaten
bashful	battled	beater
basic	battleship	beatific
basically	bawl	beatification
basilica	bawled	beatify
basilisk	bayberry	beatings
basin	bayonet	beatitude
basis	bayou	beau
bask	bazaar	beauteous
basket	be	beautiful
bas-relief	beach	beautifully
bass	beacon	beautify
bassinet	bead	beauty
basso	beaded	beaver
bassoon	beadle	becalm
basswood	beadwork	became
baste	beagle	because
bastinado	beak	beckon

22

beckoned	beforehand	belfry
becloud	befriend	Belgian
become	befuddle	belie
becomingly	beg	belief
bed	beget	believable
bedbug	beggar	believe
bedchamber	begged	belittle
bedeck	begin	belittled
bedevil	begone	belittlingly
bedfellow	begonia	bell
bedizen	begot	belladonna
bedlam	begrime	bellboy
bedpost	beguile	bellicose
bedridden	beguiled	bellicosity
bedroom	begun	belligerence
bedside	behalf	belligerency
bedspread	behave	belligerent
bedspring	behavior	belligerently
bedstead	behead	bellows
bedtime	beheadings	belong
bee	beheld	belonged
beech	behemoth	belongings
beef	behest	beloved
beefsteak	behind	below
beer	behold	belt
beeswax	beholden	belted
beetle	beholder	belvedere
befall	beige	bemused
befit	bejewel	bench
befog	belch	bend
before	beleaguered	bended

23

beneath	besides	bewildered
benediction	besiege	bewilderment
benefaction	bespangle	bewitch
benefactor	bespeak	beyond
benefactress	Bessemer	bezel
benefice	best	biannual
beneficence	bestial	biannually
beneficent	bestiality	bias
beneficial	bestow	biased
beneficiary	bestowed	bibelot
benefit	bestride	Bible
benevolence	bet	Biblical
benevolent	betake	bibliographical
benighted	betimes	bibliography
benignancy	betrayal	bibulous
benignant	betrayer	bicameral
benignity	betroth	bicarbonate
bent	betrothal	bicentenary
benzene	better	biceps
bequeath	bettered	bichloride
bequest	betterment	bichromate
bereave	between	bicuspid
bereaved	betwixt	bicycle
berry	bevel	bid
berth	beveled	bidder
beryl	beverage	bide
beseech	bevy	biennial
beseeched	bewail	bier
beseechingly	bewailed	bifocal
beset	beware	big
beside	bewilder	bigamist

24

bigamous	bimetallist	birthright
bigamy	bimonthly	biscuit
bigger	binary	bisect
biggest	binder	bishop
bighorn	bindery	bishopric
bight	bindingly	bismuth
bigot	bindings	bison
bigoted	bindweed	bisque
bigotry	binnacle	bit
bijou	binocular	bite
bilateral	binomial	biter
bile	biographer	bitingly
bilge	biographic	bitten
biliary	biographical	bitter
bilingual	biographically	bitterly
bilious	biography	bittern
bilk	biological	bitterness
bill	biologically	bitters
billboard	biologist	bitumen
billed	biology	bituminous
billhead	biopsy	bivouac
billiards	biplane	bizarre
billings	bipolar	black
billion	birch	blackball
billionaire	bird	blackberry
billow	birdlime	blackbird
billowy	birdman	blackboard
billposter	birth	blacken
billsticker	birthday	blacker
bimetallic	birthmark	blackest
bimetallism	birthplace	blackfish

blackhead	blatant	blistered
blackish	blaze	blisteringly
blackjack	blazer	blistery
blackmail	blazon	blithe
blackness	bleach	blithely
blacksmith	bleacher	blithesome
bladder	bleak	blizzard
blade	bleat	bloat
blame	bleed	block
blamed	blemish	blockade
blameless	blench	blockhead
blameworthy	blend	blockhouse
blanch	blended	blond
bland	blendings	blood
blandish	bless	blooded
blandly	blessedness	bloodier
blandness	blessings	bloodiest
blank	blew	bloodless
blanker	blight	bloodletting
blankest	blimp	bloodroot
blanket	blind	bloodshed
blankly	blinded	bloodshot
blare	blinder	bloodstain
blared	blindfold	bloody
blarney	blindly	bloom
blaspheme	blink	bloomed
blasphemed	blinker	bloomer
blasphemous	bliss	blossom
blasphemy	blissful	blossomed
blast	blissfully	blot
blasted	blister	blotch

26

blotter	blustered	bola
blouse	blusteringly	bold
blow	boa	boldly
blower	boar	boldness
blowfish	board	bolero
blowgun	boarded	boll
blowhole	boarder	bolo
blown	boast	bolometer
blowpipe	boaster	bolster
blowtorch	boastful	bolstered
blowy	boastfully	bolt
blubber	boat	bolted
bludgeon	boatswain	bolthead
blue	bobbin	bolus
bluefish	bobolink	bomb
bluestocking	bobtail	bombard
bluff	bode	bombarded
blunder	bodice	bombardier
blunderbuss	bodily	bombard-ment
blundered	bodkin	bombast
blunderingly	body	bombastic
blunt	bog	bomber
blunted	boggle	bombings
bluntly	boggled	bombproof
bluntness	bogus	bombshell
blur	Bohemian	bonanza
blurred	boil	bonbon
blurt	boiled	bond
blush	boiler	bondage
blushingly	boisterous	bonded
bluster	boisterously	bondholder

27

bondman	boomerang	borough
bondsman	boon	borrow
bone	boorish	borrowed
boned	boost	borrowings
boneless	boosted	bosky
boneset	booster	bosom
bonfire	boot	boss
bonito	bootblack	botanic
bonnet	booted	botanical
bonus	bootee	botanist
booby	booth	botanize
boodle	bootjack	botany
book	bootleg	botch
bookbinder	bootlegger	both
bookings	bootless	bother
bookish	booty	bothersome
bookkeeper	booze	bottle
bookkeeping	boracic	bottled
booklet	borate	bottom
booklets	borax	bottomless
bookmaker	Bordeaux	bottomry
bookmark	border	botulism
bookplate	bordered	boudoir
bookrack	bore	bough
bookseller	bored	bought
bookshelf	boredom	boulder
bookshop	borer	boulevard
bookstore	boric	bounce
bookworm	borings	bouncer
boom	born	bound
boomed	boron	boundary

28

bounded	boysenberry	brave
bounden	brace	braver
boundless	bracelet	bravery
bounteous	bracelets	bravest
bounteously	bracket	bravo
bountiful	bracketed	brawl
bounty	brackish	brawler
bouquet	bradawl	brawny
bourgeois	brag	brazen
bout	braid	brazier
bovine	braided	breach
bow	Braille	bread
bow	brain	breadfruit
bower	brainless	breadth
bowknot	brainy	breadwinner
bowl	braise	break
bowlder	brake	breakable
bowled	brakeman	breakage
bowlegged	bramble	breakdown
bowman	bran	breakfast
bowshot	branch	breakneck
bowsprit	brand	breakwater
box	branded	breast
boxed	brandied	breastbone
boxer	brandish	breastpin
boxwood	brandy	breastplate
boy	brash	breastwork
boycott	brass	breath
boyhood	brassard	breathless
boyish	brassy	breech
boyishness	bravado	breed

29

breeder	brigand	brittle
breeze	brigandage	brittleness
brethren	brigantine	broach
breve	bright	broad
brevet	brighten	broadcast
breviary	brighter	broaden
brevier	brightest	broader
brevity	brightly	broadest
brew	brightness	broadloom
brewery	brilliance	broadly
bribe	brilliant	broadside
bribed	brilliantly	brocade
bribery	brim	brocatel
brick	brimful	broccoli
brickbat	brimstone	brochette
bricklayer	brindled	brochure
brickyard	brine	brogan
bridal	bring	brogue
bride	brink	broil
bridge	briny	broiled
bridgehead	briquette	broiler
bridle	brisk	broke
bridled	brisket	broken
brief	bristle	brokenly
briefer	bristled	broker
briefest	bristly	brokerage
briefly	Britannia	bromate
brier	Britannic	bromide
brig	British	bromine
brigade	Britisher	bronchial
brigadier	Briton	bronchitis

30

bronze	brute	bugle
brood	brutish	bugler
brooded	bubble	build
brooder	bubonic	builder
brook	buccal	buildings
brooklet	buccaneer	built
brooklets	buck	bulb
broom	buckboard	bulbous
broth	bucket	bulge
brother	bucketful	bulged
brotherhood	buckle	bulk
brother-in-law	buckled	bulkhead
brotherly	buckler	bulkiest
brougham	buckram	bulky
brought	bucksaw	bull
brow	buckshot	bullet
brown	buckskin	bulletin
browse	buckwheat	bullfight
bruin	bucolic	bullfinch
bruise	bud	bullfrog
bruised	budge	bullhead
bruit	budged	bullion
brunette	budget	bullish
brunt	budgetary	bullock
brush	buff	bully
brushwood	buffalo	bullyrag
brusque	buffer	bulrush
brutal	buffoon	bulwark
brutality	buffoonery	bum
brutalize	bug	bumboat
brutally	bugbear	bump

31

bumper	burin	butler
bumpier	burlap	butt
bumpiest	burlesque	butter
bumpkin	burly	butterball
bumpy	burn	buttercup
buna	burned	buttered
bunch	burner	butterfat
bundle	burnish	butterfly
bundled	burnt	butternut
bung	burr	butterscotch
bungalow	burro	buttery
bungle	burrow	button
bungled	bursar	buttonhole
bungler	burst	buttonholed
bunion	bury	buttress
bunker	bus	buxom
buoy	bush	buy
buoyant	bushings	buyer
buoyantly	busily	buzz
burden	business	buzzard
burdensome	businesslike	buzzer
bureau	buskin	by
bureaucracy	bust	bygone
bureaucrat	bustard	bypass
burette	bustle	bypath
burgee	bustled	byplay
burgeon	busy	by-product
burgess	busybody	Byronic
burglar	but	bystander
burglary	butcher	byway
burial	butchery	byword

32

C

cab	caffeine	caliber
cabal	cage	calibrate
cabbage	caged	calibration
cabin	cairn	calico
cabinet	caitiff	caliper
cable	cajole	calisthenics
cablegram	cajolery	calk
caboose	cake	call
cacao	cakewalk	calla
cachalot	calabash	called
cache	calamitous	caller
cachet	calamitously	calligraphy
cackle	calamity	calliope
cackled	calcification	callosity
cactus	calcify	callous
cadaver	calcimine	calloused
cadaverous	calcine	callously
caddie	calcined	callow
cadence	calcium	callowly
cadenza	calculate	callus
cadet	calculated	calm
cadmium	calculation	calmer
Cadmus	calculator	calmest
cadre	caldron	calmly
caduceus	calendar	calmness
cafe	calf	calomel
cafeteria	calfskin	caloric

33

calorie	canceled	canoe
calumniate	cancellation	canon
calumniated	cancer	canonical
calumniation	cancerous	canonicals
calumniator	candelabrum	canonize
calumny	candid	canopy
Calvary	candidacy	can't
calved	candidate	cant
calyx	candidly	cantaloupe
camber	candied	cantankerous
cambium	candle	cantata
cambric	candled	canteen
came	candlefish	canter
camel	candlelight	canticle
cameleer	candlenut	cantilever
Camelot	candlestick	cantle
cameo	candor	canto
camera	candy	canton
camomile	cane	cantor
camouflage	canine	canvas
camp	canister	caoutchouc
campaign	canker	capabilities
campanile	cankerous	capability
camper	cannery	capable
camphor	cannibal	capably
camphorate	cannibalism	capacious
campus	cannily	capacitate
can	cannon	capacitated
canal	cannonade	capacity
canary	cannoneer	cape
cancel	canny	caper

34

caperings	captured	cardboard
capillarity	car	cardiac
capillary	carabineer	cardinal
capital	caracole	cardiograph
capitalism	caracoled	cardiology
capitalist	carafe	carditis
capitalists	caramel	care
capitalization	caramelize	cared
capitalize	carapace	careen
capitalized	carat	careened
capitulate	caravan	career
capitulated	caravansary	careful
capitulates	caravel	carefully
capitulation	caraway	carefulness
caprice	carbide	careless
capricious	carbine	carelessly
capsize	carbohydrate	carelessness
capstan	carbolic	caress
capsule	carbon	caressingly
captain	carbonate	caret
captaincy	carbonic	carfare
caption	carboniferous	cargo
captious	carbonize	caribou
captiously	carbonized	caricature
captiousness	carborundum	caricatured
captivate	carboy	caries
captivated	carbuncle	carillon
captivation	carburetor	carminative
captive	carcass	carmine
captivity	carcinoma	carnage
capture	card	carnal

35

carnally

carnation

carnelian

carnival

carnivorous

carol

caroled

carom

caromed

carotid

carouse

caroused

carp

carpal

carpenter

carpet

carpeted

carriage

carrier

carrion

carrot

carrousel

carry

cart

cartage

carted

cartel

cartilage

cartilaginous

cartography

carton

cartoon

cartouche

cartridge

carve

carved

carver

caryatid

cascade

case

casein

casement

cash

cashed

cashier

cashmere

casino

cask

casket

cassation

cassava

casserole

cassia

cassock

cast

castanet

caste

caster

castigate

castigated

castigation

castle

castoff

castor

castrametation

casual

casually

casualty

casuist

casuistry

cataclysm

catacomb

catafalque

Catalan

catalepsy

cataleptic

catalogue

catalpa

catalysis

catalytic

catalyze

catamount

catapult

cataract

catarrh

catarrhal

catastrophe

catastrophic

Catawba

catbird

catboat

catch

catcher

36

catchword	causeway	celebrate
catchy	caustic	celebrated
catechism	cauterization	celebration
catechize	cauterize	celebrity
categorical	cauterized	celerity
category	cautery	celery
catenary	caution	celesta
cater	cautionary	celestial
catered	cautious	celestially
caterer	cavalcade	celibacy
caterpillar	cavalier	celibate
catfish	cavalry	cell
catgut	cave	cellar
cathedral	caveat	cellarer
catheter	cavern	cellaret
catheterize	cavernous	cellist
cathode	caviar	cello
catholic	cavil	cellophane
catholicism	cavity	cellular
catholicity	cavort	cellulitis
catnip	cayenne	celluloid
cattle	cease	cellulose
caucus	ceased	Celtic
caudal	ceaseless	cement
caught	cecum	cementation
causal	cedar	cemetery
causality	cede	cenobite
causation	ceded	cenotaph
causative	cedilla	censer
cause	ceilings	censor
causeless	celebrant	censorial

censorious	cerebral	chained
censorship	cerebrum	chainwork
censurable	cerement	chair
censure	ceremonial	chairman
censured	ceremonially	chaise
census	ceremonious	chalcedony
cent	ceremoniously	chalet
centaur	ceremoniousness	chalice
centenarian	ceremony	chalk
centenary	cerise	chalkiness
centennial	cerium	challenge
center	certain	challenged
centerboard	certainly	chamber
centered	certainty	chambered
centerpiece	certificate	chamberlain
centigrade	certification	chambermaid
centimeter	certify	chameleon
centipede	certiorari	chamois
central	certitude	champagne
centralization	cervical	champion
centralize	cervix	championship
centralized	cesium	chance
centrally	cessation	chanced
centrifugal	cession	chancel
centripetal	cesspool	chancellery
century	cestus	chancellor
cephalalgia	cetacean	chancery
cephalic	chafe	chandelier
ceramic	chaffinch	chandler
cereal	chagrin	chandlery
cerebellum	chain	change

38

changeable	charioteer	chatty
changeless	charitable	cheap
changeling	charitably	cheapen
channel	charity	cheapened
channeled	charlatan	cheaper
chant	charm	cheapest
chanted	charmed	cheaply
chaos	charmingly	cheapness
chaotic	chart	cheat
chapel	charted	cheated
chaperon	charter	check
chaplain	chartreuse	checked
chaplet	chary	checker
chaplets	chase	checkerboard
chapter	chasm	checkered
chapters	chassis	checkmate
char	chaste	checkrein
character	chasten	cheeky
characteristic	chastened	cheer
characteristically	chasteningly	cheered
characterization	chastise	cheerful
characterize	chastised	cheerfully
characterized	chastisement	cheerfulness
charade	chastity	cheerily
charcoal	chasuble	cheeringly
chard	chateau	cheerless
charge	chatelaine	cheerlessly
chargeable	chattel	cheery
charged	chatter	cheese
charger	chattered	cheesecake
chariot	chatterer	cheesecloth

chef	childishly	chirp
chemical	childishness	chisel
chemically	childless	chiseled
chemise	childlike	chitterling
chemist	children	chivalric
chemistry	chili	chivalrous
chemurgy	chill	chivalry
chenille	chilled	chive
cherish	chillier	chloral
cheroot	chilliest	chlorate
cherry	chillingly	chloride
cherub	chilly	chlorinate
chess	chime	chlorine
chest	chimed	chlorite
chestnut	chimera	chloroform
chevron	chimerical	chlorophyll
chew	chimney	chlorosis
chicanery	chimpanzee	chocolate
chicken	chin	choice
chicle	china	choir
chicory	chinch	choke
chide	chinchilla	choler
chief	chine	cholera
chiefly	Chinese	choleric
chieftain	chink	choose
chiffon	chintz	chop
chiffonier	chip	chophouse
chilblain	chipmunk	choral
child	chipper	chord
childhood	chirography	chorea
childish	chiropodist	chortle

40

chorus	chummy	circular
chose	chump	circularize
chosen	chunk	circulate
chowder	church	circulated
chrism	churchman	circulation
christen	churlish	circulatory
Christendom	churlishly	circumambient
christened	churn	circumference
christenings	churned	circumferential
Christian	chute	circumflex
Christianity	chutney	circumlocution
Christmas	cicada	circumlocutory
chromatics	cicatrix	circumnavigate
chrome	cicatrize	circumscribe
chromium	cider	circumscribed
chronic	cigar	circumspect
chronicle	cigarette	circumspection
chronicled	cinch	circumspectly
chronicles	cincture	circumspectness
chronological	cinder	circumstance
chronologically	cinematograph	circumstances
chronology	cinnamon	circumstantial
chronometer	cinquefoil	circumstantially
chrysalis	cion	circumstantiate
chrysanthemum	cipher	circumvent
chubbiness	circle	circumvention
chubby	circled	circus
chuck	circuit	cirrhosis
chuckle	circuitous	cirrhotic
chucklehead	circuitously	cistern
chum	circuitousness	citadel

citation	clamshell	clause
cite	clan	claustrophobia
cited	clandestine	clavichord
citizen	clang	clavicle
citizenry	clanged	claw
citizenship	clangor	clay
citrate	clank	clean
citric	clanked	cleaned
citron	clap	cleaner
city	clapper	cleanest
civic	claptrap	cleanliness
civil	claque	cleanly
civilian	claret	cleanness
civility	clarification	cleanse
civilization	clarify	cleanser
civilize	clarinet	clear
civilized	clarion	clearance
claim	clarity	cleared
claimant	clash	clearer
claimed	clasp	clearest
clairvoyance	class	clearly
clairvoyant	classic	clearness
clamant	classical	cleat
clambake	classicism	cleavage
clamber	classicist	cleave
clambered	classicists	cleaver
clammy	classification	clef
clamor	classify	cleft
clamored	classmate	clematis
clamorous	clatter	clemency
clamp	clattered	clement

42

clench	clinker	cloudy
clerestory	clip	clove
clergy	clipper	cloven
clergyman	clippings	clover
clerical	clique	clown
clerk	cloak	clowned
clever	clock	clownish
cleverer	clockwise	cloy
cleverest	clod	cloyed
cleverly	clog	club
cleverness	cloister	cluck
clew	cloistered	clump
click	clonic	clumsier
client	close	clumsiest
clientele	closed	clumsily
cliff	closely	clumsiness
climacteric	closeness	clumsy
climate	closer	cluster
climatic	closest	clustered
climax	closet	clutch
climb	closure	clutter
climbed	clot	cluttered
climber	clothe	coach
clinch	clothes	coachman
clincher	clothespin	coadjutor
cling	clothier	coagulate
clingingly	clotted	coagulated
clinic	cloud	coagulates
clinical	cloudiness	coagulation
clinician	cloudless	coagulative
clink	clouds	coal

43

coalesce	cockpit	cogitation
coalescence	cockroach	cogitative
coalescent	cocksure	cognac
coalition	cocksureness	cognate
coalsack	cocktail	cognizance
coarse	cocoa	cognizant
coarsen	cocoon	cognomen
coarsened	code	cohabit
coarser	coded	cohere
coarsest	codefendant	cohered
coast	codeine	coherence
coastal	codex	coherent
coaster	codfish	coherently
coastwise	codicil	coherer
coat	codification	cohesion
coatings	codify	cohesive
coauthor	coeducation	cohesiveness
coax	coefficient	cohort
coaxed	coerce	coif
coaxial	coerced	coiffure
coaxingly	coercion	coign
cobalt	coercive	coil
cobble	coeval	coiled
cobra	coexecutor	coin
cobweb	coffee	coinage
cocaine	coffer	coincide
coccyx	coffin	coincidence
cochineal	cogency	coincidental
cockade	cogent	coined
cockatoo	cogitate	coiner
cockney	cogitated	coinsurance

44

coinsure	collision	columbine
coinsurer	collocation	column
coke	collodion	columnar
colander	colloid	coma
cold	colloidal	comatose
colder	colloquial	comb
coldest	colloquy	combat
coldly	collotype	combatant
colic	collusion	combative
colitis	collusive	combed
collaborate	cologne	combination
collaboration	colon	combine
collapse	colonel	combings
collar	colonial	combust
collate	colonist	combustible
collated	colonization	combustion
collateral	colonize	come
collation	colonized	comedian
colleague	colonnade	comedy
collect	colony	comeliness
collected	colophon	comely
collectible	color	comestible
collection	coloration	comet
collective	colored	comfit
collector	colorings	comfort
college	colorless	comfortable
collegiate	colossal	comfortably
collide	Colosseum	comforted
collided	colossus	comforter
collie	colporteur	comic
collier	colt	comical

comings

comma

command

commandeer

commander

commandingly

commandment

commando

commemorate

commemorated

commemoration

commemorative

commence

commenced

commencement

commend

commendable

commendation

commendatory

commended

commensurable

commensurate

comment

commentary

commentator

commented

commerce

commercial

commercialism

commercialization

commercialize

comminatory

commingle

commingled

comminute

comminuted

comminution

commiserate

commiseration

commissariat

commissary

commission

commissioned

commissioner

commit

commitment

committed

committee

commodious

commodity

commodore

common

commonalty

commoner

commonest

commonly

commonplace

commonwealth

commotion

communal

commune

communicable

communicant

communicate

communication

communicative

communion

communism

communist

communistic

community

communize

commutation

commutator

commute

commuted

commuter

compact

companion

companionable

companionship

companionway

company

comparability

comparable

comparative

compare

compared

comparison

compartment

compass

compassion

compassionate

46

compassionately	complaisant	composure
compatible	complement	compote
compatriot	complemental	compound
compeer	complementary	comprehend
compel	complemented	comprehended
compelled	complete	comprehensibility
compellingly	completed	comprehensible
compend	completion	comprehension
compendious	complex	comprehensive
compendium	complexion	compress
compensate	complexity	compressibility
compensation	compliance	compressible
compensatory	compliant	compression
compete	complicate	compressor
competence	complicated	comprise
competent	complication	compromise
competently	complicity	compromisingly
competition	complied	comptometer
competitive	compliment	comptroller
competitor	complimentary	compulsion
compilation	complin	compulsory
compile	comply	compunction
compiled	component	computation
complacence	comport	compute
complacency	compose	computed
complacent	composed	comrade
complain	composer	concatenation
complainant	composite	concave
complained	composition	concavity
complainingly	compositor	conceal
complaint	compost	concealed

47

concealment	conclude	conditional
concede	concluded	conditionally
conceit	conclusion	condole
conceited	conclusive	condolence
conceitedly	conclusively	condonation
conceivable	concoct	condone
conceivably	concoction	condoned
conceive	concomitant	condor
conceived	concord	conducive
concentrate	concordance	conduct
concentration	concourse	conducted
concentric	concrete	conduction
concept	concur	conductivity
conception	concurred	conductor
conceptual	concurrence	conduit
concern	concurrent	condyle
concerned	concussion	cone
concert	condemn	confection
concerted	condemnation	confectioner
concertina	condemnatory	confectionery
concession	condemned	confederacy
concessionaire	condensation	confederate
conch	condense	confederation
conciliate	condensed	confer
conciliated	condenser	conferee
conciliation	condescend	conference
conciliatory	condescendingly	conferred
concise	condescension	confess
concisely	condign	confessedly
conciseness	condiment	confession
conclave	condition	confessional

48

confessor	confound	congregation
confide	confounded	congregational
confided	confrere	congress
confidence	confront	congressional
confident	confrontation	congruence
confidential	confronted	congruent
confidentially	confuse	congruity
confidently	confused	congruous
confidingly	confusedly	conic
configuration	confusingly	conical
confine	confusion	coniferous
confined	confutation	conjectural
confinement	confute	conjecture
confirm	confuted	conjectured
confirmation	congeal	conjugal
confirmed	congealed	conjugate
confiscate	congenial	conjugated
confiscated	congeniality	conjugation
confiscation	congenially	conjunction
confiscatory	congenital	conjunctive
conflagration	congest	conjunctivitis
conflict	congestion	conjuration
confliction	conglomerate	conjure
confluence	conglomeration	conjured
confluent	congratulate	conjurer
conform	congratulated	connect
conformable	congratulates	connectedly
conformation	congratulation	connecter
conformed	congratulatory	connection
conformer	congregate	connective
conformity	congregated	connivance

49

connive

connoisseur

connotation

connote

connubial

conquer

conquered

conqueror

conquest

conquests

consanguinity

conscience

conscientious

conscientiously

conscious

consciously

consciousness

conscript

consecrate

consecrated

consecration

consecutive

consensus

consent

consented

consequence

consequent

consequential

consequently

conservation

conservatism

conservative

conservatory

conserve

conserved

consider

considerable

considerate

consideration

considers

consign

consigned

consignee

consignment

consignor

consist

consistency

consistent

consistory

consists

consolation

console

consoled

consolidate

consolidated

consolidation

consolingly

consols

consonance

consonant

consonantal

consort

consorted

conspicuous

conspicuously

conspiracy

conspirator

conspiratorial

conspire

conspired

constable

constabulary

constancy

constant

constantly

constellation

consternation

constipation

constituency

constituent

constitute

constituted

constitution

constitutional

constitutionality

constitutionally

constrain

constrained

constraint

constrict

constriction

construct

constructed

constructive	contemptible	continuous
construe	contemptuous	continuously
construed	contend	continuum
consul	contended	contort
consular	contender	contorted
consulate	content	contortion
consulates	contented	contortionist
consult	contention	contour
consultant	contentious	contraband
consultation	contentment	contrabass
consultative	contest	contract
consulted	contestant	contracted
consumable	contestation	contractile
consume	contests	contraction
consummate	context	contractor
consummation	contextual	contradict
consumption	contiguity	contradiction
consumptive	contiguous	contradictory
contact	continence	contradis-
contagion	continent	tinction
contagious	continental	contraindicate
contain	contingency	contralto
contained	contingent	contraption
container	continual	contrary
contaminate	continually	contrast
contamination	continuance	contrasts
contemplate	continuant	contravene
contemplation	continuation	contravention
contemporaneous	continue	contribute
contemporary	continued	contribution
contempt	continuity	contributor
		contributory

contrite	conventionality	convocation
contritely	conventionalize	convoke
contrition	conventionally	convoked
contrivance	conventual	convolution
contrive	converge	convoy
control	convergence	convoyed
controllable	convergent	convulse
controlled	conversant	convulsion
controller	conversation	convulsive
controversial	conversational	cooker
controversy	conversationalist	cookery
controvert	converse	cool
contumacious	conversion	cooled
contumacy	convert	cooler
contumely	converted	coolest
contuse	convertibility	coolie
contusion	convertible	coolly
conundrum	convex	coolness
convalesce	convexity	coop
convalescence	convey	cooper
convalescent	conveyance	cooperage
convection	conveyed	co-operate
convene	conveyor	co-operation
convened	convict	co-operative
convenience	convicted	co-opt
conveniences	conviction	co-ordinate
convenient	convince	co-ordination
conveniently	convincingly	copartner
convent	convivial	copartnership
convention	conviviality	Copernican
conventional	convivially	copious

52

copiously	cornered	corresponds
copiousness	cornice	corridor
copper	cornucopia	corroborate
copperhead	corona	corroboration
copperplate	coroner	corroborative
coppersmith	coronet	corroboratory
copra	corporal	corrode
copy	corporate	corroded
copyright	corporately	corrosion
coracle	corporation	corrosive
coral	corporeal	corrugate
cord	corps	corrugation
cordage	corpse	corrupt
corded	corpulence	corrupted
cordial	corpulent	corruptible
cordiality	corpuscle	corruption
cordially	corpuscular	corruptly
cordite	corral	corsage
cordon	correct	corsair
Cordovan	correction	corset
corduroy	corrective	cortege
core	correctly	cortex
cored	correctness	cortical
corespondent	corrector	corundum
Corinthian	correlate	coruscate
cork	correlation	coruscation
corkscrew	correlative	coryza
cormorant	correspond	cosily
corn	correspondence	cosine
cornea	correspondent	cosiness
corner	correspondingly	cosmetic

cosmic	counterfeit	courthouse
cosmopolitan	counterfeiter	courtier
cosmos	counterirritant	courtliness
Cossack	countermand	courtly
cost	countermine	courtship
costliness	counterpart	courtyard
costly	counterplot	cousin
costume	counterpoint	cove
costumer	countershaft	covenant
coterie	countersign	cover
cottage	countersink	coverage
cotter	counterweight	coverlet
cotton	countess	coverlets
cottontail	countless	covert
couch	country	covet
cougar	county	covetous
cough	coupé	coward
could	couple	cowardice
council	coupler	cowardly
councilor	couplet	cowboy
counsel	couplets	cowcatcher
counseled	couplings	cowl
count	coupon	cowlick
counted	courage	coworker
countenance	courageous	coxcomb
counter	courier	coy
counteract	course	coyly
counterbalance	courser	coyness
countercharge	court	coyote
countercheck	courteous	crab
countered	courtesy	crack

54

cracker	crass	creator
crackle	crate	creature
crackled	crated	credence
cradle	crater	credential
cradled	cravat	credibility
craft	crave	credible
craftier	craven	credit
craftiest	cravenette	creditable
craftily	cravings	credited
craftiness	crawfish	creditor
craftsman	crawl	credo
crafty	crawled	credulity
crag	crayon	credulous
cram	craze	creed
crammed	crazier	creek
cramp	craziest	creep
cranberry	crazily	creeper
crane	craziness	creepiness
craned	crazy	cremate
cranial	creak	cremated
craniotomy	creakingly	cremation
cranium	cream	crematory
crank	creamery	Cremona
crankcase	creamier	creole
cranked	creamiest	creosote
crankily	creamy	crepitant
crankiness	crease	crepitate
cranky	create	crescendo
cranny	created	crescent
crape	creation	crest
crash	creative	crestfallen

55

cretin	criticize	crowbar
cretonne	criticized	crowd
crevasse	critique	crowded
crevice	croak	crown
crew	croaker	crowned
crewel	croakingly	crucial
crib	crochet	crucially
cribbage	crock	crucible
cricket	crockery	crucifixion
crime	crocodile	cruciform
criminal	crocus	crude
criminally	crook	crudity
criminology	crooked	cruel
crimp	croon	cruelly
crimson	crooned	cruelty
cringe	crooner	cruise
crinkle	crop	cruiser
crinoline	croquet	crumb
cripple	croquette	crumble
crises	crosier	crumpet
crisis	cross	crumple
crisp	crossbar	crumpled
crisply	crossbow	crunch
crispness	crosscut	crusade
crisscross	crossings	crusader
criteria	crossroad	cruse
criterion	crosswise	crush
critic	crotchet	crushingly
critical	crouch	crust
critically	croup	crusty
criticism	crow	crutch

56

crux	cull	curacy
cry	culled	curare
cryolite	culminate	curate
crypt	culminated	curative
cryptic	culmination	curator
cryptical	culpability	curb
cryptically	culpable	curbed
cryptogram	culprit	curd
cryptograph	cult	cure
cryptography	cultivate	cured
crystal	cultivated	curette
crystalline	cultivation	curfew
crystallization	cultivator	curio
crystallize	cultural	curiosities
crystallized	culturally	curiosity
cub	culture	curious
cube	cultured	curiously
cubeb	culvert	curl
cubic	cumbersome	curled
cubicle	cumulative	curler
cubit	cuneiform	curlicue
cuckoo	cunningly	curly
cucumber	cupboard	curmudgeon
cuddle	cupel	currant
cuddled	cupellation	currency
cudgel	cupful	current
cue	Cupid	currently
cuff	cupidity	curricula
cuirass	cupola	curriculum
cuisine	cur	curse
culinary	curable	cursive

cursory	cute	cyclopedic
curt	cuticle	Cyclops
curtail	cutlass	cyclotron
curtain	cutlery	cygnet
curtly	cutlet	cylinder
curvature	cutlets	cylindric
curve	cutout	cylindrical
curved	cutter	cymbal
cushion	cuttings	cynic
cusp	cuttlefish	cynical
cuspidor	cyanate	cynically
custard	cyanic	cynicism
custodial	cyanide	cynosure
custodian	cyanite	cypress
custody	cyanogen	cyst
custom	cyanosis	cystitis
customarily	cycle	cystoid
customary	cyclometer	cystolith
customer	cyclone	cystotomy
cut	cyclonic	czar
cutaneous	cyclopedia	Czech

D

dachshund
dacoit
daedal
daffodil
daft
dagger
daguerreotype
dahlia
daily
daintier
daintiest
daintily
daintiness
dainty
dairy
dairyman
dais
daisy
dalliance
dally
dalmatian
dam
damage
damaged
damascene
damascus
damask

dammed
damnable
damp
dampen
dampened
damper
dampest
dampness
dance
dancer
dandelion
dandle
dandled
dandruff
dandy
danger
dangerous
dangerously
dangle
dangled
Danish
dank
dapper
dapple
dappled
dare
dared

daringly
dark
darken
darker
darkest
darkly
darkness
darling
dart
dash
dastardly
data
date
dated
dative
datum
daub
daughter
daughter-in-law
daunt
daunted
dauntless
dauphin
davenport
davit
dawdle
dawdled

59

dawn	dearer	decade
dawned	dearest	decadence
day	dearly	decadent
daybook	dearth	decalcomania
daybreak	death	decant
daydream	deathbed	decanter
daylight	deathblow	decapitate
daytime	deathless	decapitation
dazzle	deathly	decathlon
dazzled	debacle	decay
dazzlingly	debar	decease
deacon	debark	decedent
dead	debarred	deceit
deaden	debase	deceitful
deadened	debased	deceive
deadfall	debasement	deceived
deadhead	debatable	deceleration
deadlock	debate	December
deadly	debated	decency
deaf	debater	decennial
deafen	debauch	decent
deafened	debauchery	decently
deafeningly	debenture	decen-
deafer	debilitate	tralization
deafest	debilitated	decentralize
deal	debility	deception
dealer	debit	deceptive
dealings	debited	deceptively
dean	debt	decide
deanery	debtor	decidedly
dear	debut	deciduous
60		decimal

decimate	decoration	deepen
decimation	decorative	deepened
decipher	decorator	deeper
decipherable	decorous	deepest
deciphered	decorously	deeply
decision	decorum	deepness
decisive	decoy	deer
decisively	decrease	deerskin
decisiveness	decreased	deface
deck	decreasingly	defacement
deckle	decree	defalcate
declaim	decrepitude	defalcated
declamation	decretal	defalcation
declamatory	decried	defamation
declaration	decry	defamatory
declarative	dedicate	defame
declaratory	dedicated	defamed
declare	dedication	default
declared	dedicatory	defaulter
declension	deduce	defeasible
declination	deduced	defeat
decline	deducible	defect
declined	deduct	defection
declivity	deductible	defective
decoction	deduction	defend
decompose	deductively	defendant
decomposition	deed	defended
decontaminate	deeded	defender
decontamination	deem	defense
decorate	deemed	defensible
decorated	deep	defensive

61

defensively	deformation	delay
defer	deformed	delectable
deference	deformity	delectation
deferential	defraud	delegate
deferment	defrauded	delegated
deferred	defray	delegation
defiance	defrayed	delete
defiant	deft	deleted
defiantly	deftly	deleterious
deficiency	defunct	deletion
deficient	defy	delftware
deficit	degeneracy	deliberate
defilade	degenerate	deliberation
defile	degenerately	deliberative
defiled	degeneration	delicacy
defilement	degradation	delicate
define	degrade	delicately
defined	degraded	delicatessen
definite	degradingly	delicious
definitely	degree	deliciously
definiteness	dehydrate	delight
definition	dehydration	delightful
definitive	deification	delightfully
definitively	deify	delimit
deflate	deign	delimitation
deflated	deigned	delineate
deflect	deism	delineated
deflected	deist	delineation
deflection	deity	delineator
deforestation	dejectedly	delinquency
deform	dejection	delinquent

62

deliquesce

deliquescence

deliquescent

delirious

delirium

deliver

deliverance

deliverer

delivery

delphinium

delta

delude

deluded

deluge

delusion

delusive

de luxe

delve

demagnetize

demagogue

demand

demandingly

demarcation

demean

demeanor

demented

dementia

demerit

demigod

demise

demobilization

demobilize

demobilized

democracy

democrat

democratic

democratically

democratize

demolish

demolished

demolition

demon

demonetization

demonetize

demonstrable

demonstrate

demonstration

demonstrative

demonstrator

demoralization

demoralize

demoralized

demotic

demountable

demur

demure

demurely

demurrage

demurred

demurrer

den

denature

denatured

denial

denied

denizen

denominate

denominated

denomination

denominational

denotation

denote

denoted

denounce

dense

density

dent

dental

dentalgia

dented

dentifrice

dentist

dentistry

dentition

denunciation

denunciatory

deny

deodorant

deodorize

deodorized

depart

department

departmental

departure	depravation	dereliction
depend	deprave	deride
depended	depravity	derision
dependency	deprecate	derisive
dependent	deprecated	derivation
depict	deprecation	derivative
depiction	deprecatingly	derive
depilatory	deprecatory	dermal
deplete	depreciate	dermatitis
depleted	depreciated	dermatology
depletion	depreciation	derogatory
deplorable	depredation	derrick
deplore	depress	dervish
deplored	depressant	descend
deploy	depressingly	descendant
deployment	depression	descent
depolarization	depressive	describe
depolarize	deprivation	described
depopulate	deprive	description
deport	depth	descriptive
deportation	deputation	descry
deportment	depute	desecrate
depose	deputed	desecrated
deposed	deputize	desecration
deposit	deputy	desensitize
depositary	derail	desert
deposited	derailment	desertion
deposition	derange	deserve
depositor	deranged	deserved
depository	derangement	deservedly
depot	derelict	desiccant

64

desiccate	despoil	detained
desiccator	despoiled	detect
desiderata	despondency	detection
desideratum	despondent	detective
design	despot	detector
designate	despotic	detention
designated	despotism	deter
designation	desquamated	detergent
designed	desquamation	deteriorate
designer	dessert	deterioration
desirability	destination	determinable
desirable	destine	determination
desire	destined	determinative
desires	destiny	determine
desirous	destitute	determined
desist	destitution	deterred
desists	destroy	deterrent
desk	destroyer	detest
desolate	destructible	detestable
desolately	destruction	detestation
desolation	destructive	detests
despair	desuetude	dethrone
despaired	desultorily	detonate
despairingly	desultory	detonated
desperate	detach	detonation
desperately	detachable	detonator
desperation	detached	detour
despicable	detachment	detoured
despise	detail	detract
despised	detailed	detraction
despite	detain	detractor

detriment	devotional	diameter
detrimental	devour	diametric
detritus	devoured	diamond
devaluate	devoutly	diapason
devaluated	dew	diaper
devaluation	dewy	diaphanous
devastate	dexter	diaphanously
devastated	dexterity	diaphragm
devastation	dexterous	diastole
develop	dexterously	diastolic
development	dextrose	diathermic
developmental	diabetes	diatom
deviate	diabetic	diatonic
deviated	diabolic	diatribe
deviation	diabolical	dice
device	diaconal	dichotomy
devil	diacritical	dictaphone
deviltry	diadem	dictate
devious	diaeresis	dictated
deviously	diagnose	dictation
deviousness	diagnosed	dictator
devise	diagnoses	dictatorial
devised	diagnosis	dictatorially
devitalize	diagnostic	dictatorship
devoid	diagnostician	diction
devolve	diagonal	dictionary
devolved	diagram	dictograph
devote	dial	dictum
devoted	dialect	did
devotee	dialed	didactic
devotion	dialogue	die

66

died	dignity	dine
diet	digress	dined
dietary	digression	diner
dietetics	dike	dingily
differ	dilapidate	dingy
differed	dilapidation	dinner
difference	dilatation	dinosaur
different	dilate	dint
differential	dilation	diocese
differentiate	dilatory	diopter
differentiated	dilemma	diorama
differentiation	diligence	diphtheria
difficult	diligent	diphthong
difficulty	diligently	diploma
diffidence	dilute	diplomacy
diffident	diluted	diplomat
diffract	dilution	diplomatic
diffraction	dim	diplomatist
diffuse	dime	diplopia
diffused	dimension	dipper
diffusion	dimensional	dipsomania
dig	diminish	dipsomaniac
digest	diminuendo	direct
digestible	diminution	direction
digestion	diminutive	directive
digestive	dimity	directly
diggings	dimly	directness
digit	dimmed	director
digitalis	dimmer	directorate
dignify	dimmest	directory
dignitary	dimness	direful

direst	disarrange	discipline
dirge	disarray	disciplined
dirigible	disarticulate	disclaim
dirndl	disassociate	disclaimed
dirt	disaster	disclaimer
dirtily	disastrous	disclose
dirty	disastrously	disclosure
disability	disavow	discolor
disable	disavowal	discoloration
disabuse	disband	discomfit
disadvantage	disbanded	discomfiture
disadvantageous	disbar	discomfort
disaffected	disbarment	discommode
disaffection	disbarred	discompose
disaffirm	disbelieve	discomposure
disaffirmed	disbeliever	disconcert
disagree	disbelievingly	disconnect
disagreeable	disburse	disconnected
disagreement	disbursement	disconsolate
disallow	discard	disconsolately
disappear	discarded	discontent
disappearance	discern	discontented
disappoint	discerned	discontent-
		ment
disappointingly	discernible	discontinuance
disappointment	discerningly	discontinue
disapprobation	discernment	discontinued
disapproval	discharge	discord
disarm	discharged	discordant
disarmament	disciple	discount
disarmed	discipleship	discountenance
disarmingly	disciplinary	discourage

68

discouraged	diseased	dishonored
discouragement	disembarkation	disillusion
discouragingly	disembarrass	disinclination
discourse	disembody	disincline
discourteous	disenchant	disinclined
discourtesy	disengage	disinfect
discover	disesteem	disinfectant
discoverer	disfavor	disingenuous
discovery	disfeature	disinherit
discredit	disfigure	disintegrate
discreditable	disfigured	disinterested
discredited	disfigurement	disinterestedly
discreet	disgorge	disjoin
discrepancy	disgrace	disjoined
discrete	disgraced	disjoinings
discretion	disgraceful	disjunction
discretionary	disgruntle	disjunctive
discriminate	disguise	disk
discriminated	disguised	dislike
discrimination	disgust	dislocate
discrimi-native	disgustedly	dislocated
discrimi-natory	disgustingly	dislocation
discursive	dish	dislodge
discus	dishabille	disloyal
discuss	disharmony	disloyalty
discusses	dishearten	dismal
discussion	dishevel	dismally
disdain	dishonest	dismantle
disdained	dishonestly	dismantled
disdainful	dishonor	dismast
disease	dishonorable	dismasted

dismay	dispensation	disqualification
dismayed	dispense	disqualify
dismember	dispensed	disquiet
dismembered	dispersal	disquietude
dismemberment	disperse	disquisition
dismiss	dispersed	disregard
dismissal	dispersion	disrepair
dismount	dispirited	disreputable
dismounted	displace	disrepute
disobedience	displacement	disrespect
disobedient	display	disrespectful
disobey	displease	disrobe
disobeyed	displeasure	disroot
disoblige	disport	disrupt
disorder	disposal	disruption
disorderly	dispose	disruptive
disorganize	disposed	dissatisfaction
disown	disposition	dissatisfy
disparage	dispossess	dissect
disparagement	dispossessed	dissemble
disparagingly	disposure	disseminate
disparate	dispraise	disseminated
disparity	disproof	dissemination
dispassionate	disproportion	dissension
dispatch	disproportionate	dissent
dispatched	disputable	dissenter
dispatcher	disputant	dissentient
dispel	disputation	dissertation
dispelled	disputatious	disservice
dispensable	dispute	dissidence
dispensary	disputed	dissident

dissimilar	distilled	disturber
dissimilarity	distiller	disunion
dissimulate	distillery	disunite
dissimulated	distinct	disuse
dissimulation	distinction	ditto
dissipate	distinctive	ditty
dissipated	distinctively	diurnal
dissipation	distinctly	divagate
dissociate	distinctness	divan
dissociated	distinguish	dive
dissociation	distort	dived
dissolute	distorted	diver
dissolution	distortion	diverge
dissolve	distract	diverged
dissolved	distractingly	divergence
dissonance	distraction	divergent
dissonant	distrain	diverse
dissuade	distrained	diversification
dissuasion	distraught	diversify
distaff	distress	diversion
distal	distressingly	diversionary
distance	distribute	diversity
distant	distribution	divert
distaste	distributive	divest
distasteful	distributor	divide
distemper	district	divided
distend	distrust	dividend
distensible	distrustful	divider
distill	disturb	divination
distillate	disturbance	divine
distillation	disturbed	divined

71

divinely	dodged	domesticate
divinity	dodo	domesticated
divisibility	doe	domesticity
divisible	doeskin	domicile
division	doff	domiciliary
divisor	dog	dominance
divorce	dogcart	dominant
divorcee	doge	dominate
divorcement	dogged	dominated
divulge	doggerel	domination
divulged	dogma	domineer
dizzier	dogmatic	domineered
dizziest	dogmatism	domineeringly
dizzily	dogmatize	dominie
dizziness	dogtrot	dominion
dizzy	dogwood	domino
do	doily	donate
docile	doings	donated
docility	doldrums	donation
dock	dole	donative
docket	doled	donkey
doctor	doleful	donor
doctorate	doll	doom
doctrinaire	dollar	doomed
doctrinal	dolman	door
doctrine	dolphin	doorknob
document	dolt	doorsill
documentary	domain	doorway
documentation	dome	dope
dodder	domed	dormant
dodge	domestic	dormer

72

dormitory	dowager	dragon
dormouse	dowdier	dragoon
dorsal	dowdiest	dragooned
dory	dowdily	drain
dosage	dowdy	drainage
dose	dowel	drained
dot	doweled	drainer
dotage	down	drainpipe
dotard	downcast	drake
dote	downfall	dram
dotingly	downhearted	drama
dotted	downhill	dramatic
double	downpour	dramatics
doubly	downright	dramatist
doubt	downstairs	dramatization
doubted	downward	dramatize
doubter	downy	dramaturgy
doubtful	dowry	drape
doubtfully	doxology	draper
doubtingly	doze	drapery
doubtless	dozen	drastic
dough	drab	draw
doughboy	draft	drawback
doughnut	draftier	drawbar
doughty	draftiest	drawbridge
doughy	draftily	drawee
dour	drafty	drawer
dove	drag	drawings
dove	draggle	drawl
dovecote	draggled	drawn
dovetail	dragnet	drawplate

73

dray	dried	dropsy
drayage	drier	dross
drayman	driest	drought
dread	drift	drove
dreaded	driftwood	drown
dreadful	drill	drowned
dream	drilled	drownings
dreamed	drink	drowse
dreamier	drinkable	drowsily
dreamiest	drinker	drowsiness
dreamily	drip	drowsy
dreamless	drippings	drudge
dreamlike	drive	drudgery
dreamy	drivel	drug
drearily	driven	druggist
dreariness	driver	druid
dreary	driveway	drum
dredge	drizzle	drumhead
dredged	drizzled	drummed
dreg	droll	drunk
drench	drollery	drunkard
drenched	dromedary	drunken
dress	drone	dry
dressed	droningly	dryly
dresser	drool	dual
dressings	droolings	duality
dressmaker	droop	dubiety
dressy	drop	dubious
drew	dropper	ducal
dribble	droppings	ducat
dribbled	dropsical	duchess

duck	dully	dust
duckling	dumb	dusted
duckpin	dummy	duster
duckweed	dump	dustiness
duct	dumpling	dusty
ductile	dun	duteous
ductility	dunce	duties
dudgeon	dune	dutiful
due	dungaree	duty
duel	dungeon	dwarf
duelist	dunnage	dwarfish
duenna	dunned	dwell
duffer	dupe	dwellings
dug	duplex	dwelt
dugong	duplicate	dwindle
dugout	duplication	dwindled
duke	duplicator	dynamic
dukedom	duplicity	dynamism
dulcet	durability	dynamite
dulcimer	durable	dynamo
dull	durance	dynasty
dullard	duration	dynatron
duller	duress	dysfunction
dullest	during	dyspepsia
dullness	dusky	dyspeptic

ℰ

each

eager

eagerly

eagerness

eagle

eaglet

ear

earl

earldom

earlier

earliest

early

earmark

earn

earned

earnest

earnestly

earring

earshot

earthen

earthenware

earthly

earthquake

earthward

earthwork

earthworm

ease

eased

easel

easement

easier

easiest

easily

east

Easter

easterly

eastern

easterner

eastward

eastwardly

easy

eat

eatable

eater

eavesdrop

ebb

ebonize

ebony

ebullience

ebullient

ebullition

eccentric

eccentricity

ecchymosis

ecclesiastic

ecclesiastical

echelon

echo

éclair

éclat

eclectic

eclecticism

eclipse

eclogue

economic

economical

economically

economize

economized

economy

ecru

ecstasy

ecstatic

ecstatically

eczema

eddy

edelweiss

edge

edged

edgeways

edgewise

edgings
edibility
edible
edict
edification
edifice
edify
edit
edited
edition
editor
editorial
editorially
educable
educate
education
educational
educationally
educator
eel
efface
effacement
effect
effected
effective
effectual
effectually
effectuate
effeminacy
effeminate
effervesce

effervescence
effervescent
effete
efficacious
efficacy
efficiency
efficient
effigies
effigy
efflorescence
efflorescent
effluvia
effluvium
effort
effortless
effrontery
effulgence
effulgent
effusion
effusive
effusively
effusiveness
eggnog
eggplant
eggshell
ego
egoism
egoist
egotistic
egotistical
egregious

egress
Egyptian
eider
either
ejaculate
ejaculation
eject
ejection
ejectment
ejector
elaborate
elaborately
elaboration
elapse
elastic
elasticity
elated
elation
elbow
elbowed
elbowroom
elder
elderberry
elderly
eldest
elect
election
electioneer
elective
elector
electoral

electorate	elephant	elopement
electrical	elephantiasis	eloquence
electrically	elephantine	eloquent
electrician	elevate	eloquently
electricity	elevation	else
electrification	elevator	elsewhere
electrify	elfin	elucidate
electrocute	elicit	elucidated
electrocution	elide	elucidation
electrode	eligibility	elude
electrolier	eligible	eluded
electrolysis	eliminate	elusive
electrolytic	eliminated	emaciate
electrolytical	elimination	emaciated
electrolyze	eliminative	emaciation
electromagnet	elision	emanate
electrometer	elite	emanated
electron	elixir	emanation
electronic	Elizabethan	emancipate
electroplate	elk	emancipated
electropositive	ellipsis	emancipation
electroscope	ellipsoid	emancipator
electrotype	elliptic	emasculate
eleemosynary	elliptical	emasculation
elegance	elm	embalm
elegant	elocution	embalmer
elegy	elocutionist	embankment
element	elongate	embargo
elemental	elongated	embarkation
elementally	elongation	embarrass
elementary	elope	embarrassed

78

embarrassment	embryo	emphatic
embassy	embryonic	empire
embattle	emend	empiric
embattled	emendation	empirical
embellish	emerald	empiricism
embellishment	emerge	emplacement
ember	emergence	employ
embezzle	emergency	employee
embezzled	emergent	employer
embezzlement	emeritus	employment
embezzler	emery	emporium
embitter	emetic	empower
embittered	emigrant	empowered
emblazon	emigrate	empress
emblem	emigration	emptied
emblematic	eminence	emptily
emblematical	eminent	emptiness
embodiment	emissary	empty
embody	emission	empyema
embolden	emit	emu
emboldened	emitted	emulate
embolism	emollient	emulated
embolus	emolument	emulates
emboss	emotion	emulation
embrace	emotional	emulative
embrasure	emotionally	emulatory
embrocation	emperor	emulous
embroider	emphases	emulsification
embroidered	emphasis	emulsify
embroidery	emphasize	emulsion
embroil	emphasized	enable

79

enact	encroach	endowment
enacted	encroachment	endue
enactment	encumber	endurable
enamel	encumbered	endurance
enameled	encumbrance	endure
enamored	encyclical	endured
encamp	encyclopedia	enduringly
encampment	encyclopedic	endways
encaustic	encysted	endwise
encephalic	end	enemy
encephalitis	endanger	energetic
enchant	endangered	energies
enchanted	endear	energize
enchantingly	endeared	energized
enchantment	endeavor	energy
encircle	endeavored	enervate
encircled	ended	enervation
encirclement	endemic	enfeeble
enclave	endings	enfilade
enclose	endive	enfold
enclosure	endless	enforce
encomia	endlessly	enforceable
encomium	endlong	enforcement
encompass	endocrine	enforcer
encore	endocrinology	enfranchise
encounter	endoderm	engage
encountered	endogenous	engaged
encourage	endorse	engagement
encouraged	endorsement	engagingly
encouragement	endow	engender
encouragingly	endowed	engendered

80

engine	enlightened	entangle
engineer	enlightenment	entanglement
English	enlist	enter
Englishman	enlisted	enteralgia
engorge	enlistment	enterectomy
engorgement	enliven	entered
engrain	enlivened	enteritis
engrained	enmesh	enterotomy
engrave	enmity	enterprise
engraved	ennoble	entertain
engraver	enormity	entertained
engross	enormous	entertainer
engrossed	enough	entertainingly
engrosser	enrage	entertainment
engulf	enrapture	enthrall
enhance	enraptured	enthrone
enhancement	enrich	enthusiasm
enharmonic	enrichment	enthusiast
enigma	enroll	enthusiastic
enigmatic	enrolled	enthusiastically
enigmatical	enrollment	entice
enjoin	enshrine	enticed
enjoined	ensign	enticement
enjoy	ensilage	enticingly
enjoyable	enslave	entire
enjoyment	enslavement	entirety
enlarge	ensue	entitle
enlarged	ensure	entitled
enlargement	entablature	entity
enlarger	entail	entomb
enlighten	entailed	entombed

entombment	envoys	epizootic
entomologist	envy	epoch
entomology	enzyme	equable
entrails	eon	equably
entrance	ephemeral	equal
entrancingly	epic	equaled
entrant	epicure	equality
entrap	epicurean	equalization
entreat	epidemic	equalize
entreaty	epidermal	equalized
entrust	epidermic	equalizer
entrusted	epidermis	equally
entry	epidermoid	equanimity
entryway	epiglottis	equate
entwine	epigram	equation
enucleate	epigraph	equator
enucleation	epilepsy	equatorial
enumerate	epileptic	equerry
enumeration	epileptoid	equestrian
enumerator	epilogue	equiangular
enunciate	episcopal	equidistance
enunciation	episcopalian	equidistant
enunciator	episode	equilateral
envelope	episodic	equilibrium
enviable	epistemology	equine
envious	epistle	equinoctial
environment	epitaph	equinox
environmental	epithalamium	equip
environs	epithet	equipage
envisage	epitome	equipment
envoy	epitomize	equipoise

82

equitable	erroneous	espousal
equitation	error	espouse
equity	eructation	esprit
equivalent	erudite	espy
equivocal	erudition	esquire
equivocate	erupt	essay
equivocation	eruption	essayist
era	eruptive	essence
eradicate	erysipelas	essential
eradication	escalade	essentially
erase	escalator	establish
erased	escapade	establishment
eraser	escape	estate
erasure	escapement	esteem
erect	escarpment	esteemed
erectile	escheat	ester
erection	eschew	esthetic
erectness	escort	estimable
erg	escorted	estimate
ergo	escritoire	estimated
ergot	escrow	estimation
ermine	escutcheon	estimator
erode	Eskimo	estivate
erosion	esophagus	estoppel
err	esoteric	estrange
errand	esparto	estranged
errata	especial	estrangement
erratic	especially	estron
erratically	Esperanto	estuary
erratum	espionage	esurient
erred	esplanade	etch

83

etcher	European	eventuality
etchings	Eustachian	eventually
eternal	eutectic	eventuate
eternally	evacuate	ever
eternity	evacuated	everglade
ethane	evacuation	evergreen
ether	evade	everlasting
ethereal	evaded	everlastingly
ethereally	evaluate	every
ethical	evaluation	everybody
ethically	evanescence	everyday
ethics	evanescent	everyone
ethnology	evangelical	everything
ethyl	evangelist	everywhere
etiquette	evaporate	evict
etymological	evaporation	evicted
etymology	evaporator	eviction
eucalyptus	evasion	evidence
Eucharist	evasive	evident
euchre	evasively	evidently
Euclid	evasiveness	evidential
eugenics	even	evil
eulogistic	evening	evilly
eulogize	evenings	evince
eulogy	evenly	eviscerate
euphemism	evenness	evocation
euphemistic	event	evocative
euphonious	eventful	evoke
euphony	eventfully	evolution
Eurasian	eventual	evolutionary
eureka	eventualities	evolutionist

84

evolve	excel	exclosure
ewe	excelled	exclude
ewer	excellence	excluded
exacerbate	excellency	exclusion
exacerbation	excellent	exclusive
exact	excelsior	excommunicate
exaction	except	excommunication
exactitude	exception	excoriate
exactly	exceptional	excoriated
exactness	exceptionally	excoriation
exaggerate	excerpt	excrescence
exaggerated	excess	excrete
exaggeration	excesses	excretion
exalt	excessive	excretory
exaltation	excessively	excruciate
exalted	exchange	excruciated
examinable	exchequer	excruciatingly
examination	excipient	excruciation
examine	excise	exculpate
examined	excision	exculpated
examiner	excitability	exculpation
example	excitable	exculpatory
exasperate	excitant	excursion
exasperatingly	excitation	excusable
exasperation	excite	excuse
excavate	excitedly	excused
excavation	excitement	excuses
excavator	exclaim	execrable
exceed	exclaimed	execrate
exceeded	exclamation	execration
exceedingly	exclamatory	executant

85

execute	exhibit	expand
executed	exhibited	expanded
execution	exhibition	expanse
executioner	exhibitor	expansion
executive	exhilarate	expansive
executor	exhilaration	expatiate
executrix	exhort	expatiated
exegeses	exhortation	expatriate
exegesis	exhorted	expatriation
exemplar	exhumation	expect
exemplary	exhume	expectancy
exemplification	exigency	expectant
exemplify	exigent	expectantly
exempt	exiguous	expectation
exempted	exile	expectorant
exemption	exist	expectorate
exequatur	existence	expectoration
exercise	existent	expediency
exercised	exists	expedient
exerciser	exit	expediently
exert	exodus	expeditate
exerted	exonerate	expedite
exertion	exoneration	expedited
exhalation	exorbitant	expedition
exhale	exorbitantly	expeditionary
exhaled	exorcise	expeditious
exhaust	exorcised	expeditiously
exhaustion	exorcism	expel
exhaustive	exordium	expelled
exhaustively	exoteric	expend
exhaustless	exotic	expended

86

expenditure	exploited	expropriate
expense	exploration	expropriation
expensively	exploratory	expulsion
experience	explore	expunge
experienced	explored	expunged
experiences	explorer	expurgate
experiment	exploringly	expurgated
experimental	explosion	expurgation
experimentally	explosive	exquisite
experimentation	exponent	extant
experimenter	exponential	extemporaneous
expert	export	extempore
expertly	exportable	extemporization
expertness	exportation	extemporize
expiate	expose	extend
expiation	exposed	extended
expiration	exposition	extensible
expire	expositor	extension
expired	expository	extensive
explain	expostulate	extent
explained	expostulated	extenuate
explanation	expostulation	extenuated
explanatory	exposure	extenuation
expletive	expound	exterior
explicable	express	exterminate
explicit	expressage	exterminated
explicitly	expression	extermination
explode	expressive	exterminator
exploded	expressively	external
exploit	expressly	externally
exploitation	expressman	extinct

extinction	extraordinary	exudation
extinguish	extravagance	exude
extirpate	extravagant	exult
extirpated	extravaganza	exultant
extirpation	extravasate	exultation
extol	extravasation	exulted
extort	extreme	exultingly
extorted	extremist	eye
extortion	extremity	eyeball
extortionate	extricate	eyebrow
extra	extricated	eyelash
extract	extrication	eyeless
extraction	extrinsic	eyelet
extractive	extrude	eyelid
extradite	extruded	eyepiece
extradited	extrusion	eyes
extradition	exuberance	eyeshot
extraneous	exuberant	eyesight
extraordinarily	exudate	eyespot

F

Fabian	factual	faith
fable	factually	faithful
fabric	facultative	faithfulness
fabricate	faculties	faithless
fabrication	faculty	faithlessly
fabulous	faddist	fake
façade	fade	faker
face	faded	falcon
facet	Fahrenheit	fall
facetious	fail	fallacious
facial	failed	fallaciously
facile	failings	fallacy
facilely	faille	fallen
facilitate	failure	fallibility
facilities	faint	fallible
facility	fainted	fallow
facings	fainthearted	false
facsimile	faintly	falsehood
fact	faintness	falsely
faction	fair	falseness
factional	fairer	falsetto
factious	fairest	falsification
factitious	fairly	falsifier
factitive	fairness	falsify
factor	fairway	falsity
factory	fairy	falter
factotum	fairyland	faltered

89

falteringly	far	fat
fame	farad	fatal
famed	farce	fatalism
familial	farcical	fatalist
familiar	farcy	fatalistic
familiarity	fare	fatality
familiarize	fared	fatally
familiarly	farewell	fate
families	farina	fateful
family	farinaceous	father
famine	farm	fatherhood
famish	farmed	father-in-law
famous	farmhouse	fatherland
famously	farmyard	fatherless
fan	faro	fatherly
fanatic	farsighted	fathom
fanatical	farther	fathomless
fanaticism	farthest	fatigue
fancied	farthing	fatness
fancier	fascinate	fatten
fanciest	fascinatingly	fatter
fanciful	fashion	fattest
fancy	fashionable	fatty
fanfare	fast	fatuity
fang	fasten	fatuous
fanged	fastened	faucet
fanlight	fastenings	fault
fanned	faster	faultily
fantasia	fastest	faultless
fantastic	fastidious	faultlessly
fantasy	fastness	faulty

90

faun	federalist	felicity
fauna	federalization	feline
favor	federalize	fellow
favorable	federalized	fellowship
favored	federate	felly
favorite	federated	felon
favoritism	federation	felonious
fawn	federative	felony
fawned	fedora	felt
fealty	fee	felucca
fear	feeble	female
feared	feebleness	feminine
fearful	feeblest	femininely
fearless	feebly	femininity
fearlessly	feed	feminist
fearsome	feedback	femoral
feasibility	feedings	femur
feasible	feel	fen
feast	feeler	fence
feat	feelingly	fencer
feather	feelings	fend
featherweight	feet	fender
feathery	feign	fenestrated
feature	feigned	fenestration
featured	feint	Fenian
febrile	feldspar	fennel
February	felicitate	feral
fecund	felicitated	ferment
fecundate	felicitation	fermentation
fecundity	felicitous	fermented
federal	felicitously	fern

ferocious	festoonery	fidget
ferociously	fetch	fiduciary
ferocity	fetid	fief
ferret	fetish	field
ferreted	fetishism	fielded
ferric	fetlock	fieldpiece
ferrochrome	fetter	fiend
ferrotype	fettered	fiendish
ferrule	fettle	fiendishly
ferry	feud	fierce
ferryboat	feudal	fierceness
fertile	feudalism	fiercer
fertility	feudatory	fiercest
fertilization	fever	fiery
fertilize	feverish	fife
fertilized	feverishly	fig
ferule	few	fight
fervent	fez	figuration
fervently	fiasco	figurative
fervid	fiat	figuratively
fervidly	fib	figure
fervor	fiber	figured
fescue	fibroid	figurehead
festal	fibula	figurine
fester	fickle	filament
festered	fiction	filariasis
festival	fictional	filature
festive	fictitious	filbert
festivity	fiddle	file
festoon	fiddler	filed
festooned	fidelity	filial

92

filibuster	findings	fireside
filigree	fine	fireworks
filings	fined	firkin
fill	finely	firm
filled	fineness	firmament
filler	finer	firmer
fillet	finery	firmest
film	finespun	firmly
filmed	finesse	firmness
filmy	finest	first
filter	finger	firstly
filtered	fingered	firth
filth	fingerling	fiscal
filthier	fingerprint	fish
filthiest	finial	fisherman
filthiness	finis	fishery
filthy	finish	fishhook
filtrate	finished	fishline
filtration	finisher	fishwife
fin	finite	fishy
final	fiord	fissile
finalist	fir	fission
finality	fire	fissionable
finally	firearm	fissure
finance	firebrand	fist
financial	firebrick	fistic
financially	fired	fisticuffs
financier	firefly	fistula
finch	fireman	fit
find	fireplace	fitful
finder	fireproof	fitfully

93

fitness	flagstaff	flask
fitter	flagstone	flat
fittingly	flail	flatboat
fittings	flailed	flatfish
fix	flair	flatiron
fixation	flake	flatly
fixative	flakiness	flatness
fixed	flaky	flatten
fixings	flambeau	flatter
fixity	flamboyant	flattered
fixture	flame	flatterer
fizzle	flamed	flatteringly
fizzled	flamingly	flattery
flabbier	flamingo	flattest
flabbiest	flange	flatulence
flabbiness	flanged	flatulent
flabby	flank	flatware
flaccid	flanked	flatwise
flag	flannel	flatworm
flagellant	flannelette	flaunt
flagellate	flap	flaunted
flagellation	flapjack	flauntingly
flageolet	flare	flautist
flageolets	flared	flavor
flagitious	flash	flavored
flagon	flashboard	flavorings
flagpole	flasher	flaw
flagrance	flashily	flax
flagrant	flashiness	flaxen
flagrantly	flashingly	flay
flagship	flashy	flea

94

fleabite	flimsiness	floodlight
fleck	flimsy	floor
fledge	flinch	floppiness
fledgling	flinchingly	floppy
flee	fling	floral
fleece	flint	Florentine
fleeced	flintiness	floriculture
fleeciness	flintlock	florid
fleecy	flinty	floridly
fleet	flippancy	florin
fleetingly	flippant	florist
Flemish	flippantly	floss
flesh	flipper	flossy
fleshings	flirt	flotation
fleshy	flirtation	flotilla
Fletcherism	flirtatious	flotsam
flew	flirted	flounce
flex	flit	flounder
flexibility	flitch	floundered
flexible	flivver	flounderingly
flexure	float	flour
flick	floated	flourish
flicker	floater	flourishingly
flickeringly	flocculence	floury
flier	flocculent	flout
flight	flock	flouted
flightiness	floe	flow
flighty	flog	flower
flimsier	floggings	flowered
flimsiest	flood	floweriness
flimsily	flooded	flowerpot

95

flowery	flutings	foible
flowingly	flutist	foil
flown	flutter	foiled
fluctuate	fluttered	foist
fluctuated	flutteringly	fold
fluctuation	fluttery	folded
flue	flux	folder
fluency	fluxion	foliage
fluent	fly	foliate
fluently	flyer	foliation
fluff	flyleaf	folio
fluffiness	flytrap	folk
fluffy	flywheel	folkway
fluid	foal	follicle
fluidity	foaled	follicular
fluidly	foam	follow
fluke	foamed	followed
flume	foamier	follower
flung	foamiest	folly
flunk	foaminess	foment
flunked	foamy	fomentation
flunky	fob	fomented
fluorescence	focal	fond
fluorescent	focalize	fondant
fluorine	focus	fonder
fluoroscope	fodder	fondest
flurry	foe	fondle
flush	foeman	fondled
fluster	fog	fondly
flustered	foggy	fondness
fluted	foghorn	fondue

font	footstep	foreclosed
food	footstool	foreclosure
fool	footwear	foredeck
fooled	foozle	foredoom
foolhardy	foozled	foredoomed
foolish	foppery	forefather
foolishly	for	forefinger
foolishness	forage	forefoot
foolproof	forasmuch	forefront
foolscap	foray	foregone
foot	forbear	foreground
footage	forbearance	forehanded
football	forbid	forehead
footboard	forbidden	foreign
footbridge	forbiddingly	foreigner
footed	forebore	foreknowledge
footfall	force	foreleg
footgear	forceful	forelock
foothill	forcemeat	foreman
foothold	forceps	foremast
footings	forces	foremost
footless	forcible	forename
footlights	ford	forenoon
footman	forded	forensic
footmark	forearm	foreordain
footnote	forcbear	foreordained
footpace	forebode	forequarter
footpad	forebodings	forerunner
footpath	forecast	foresee
footprint	forecastle	foreshadow
footrest	foreclose	foreshore

97

foresight	forgo	forsythia
forest	forgot	fort
forestall	forgotten	fortalice
forestalled	fork	forth
forestation	forked	forthcoming
forested	forlorn	forthright
forester	form	forthrightness
forestry	formal	forthwith
forests	formaldehyde	fortification
foretaste	formalism	fortify
foretell	formality	fortitude
forethought	formalize	fortnight
foretold	formally	fortnightly
forever	format	fortress
forewoman	formation	fortuitous
foreword	formative	fortunate
forfeit	formed	fortune
forfeiture	former	forum
forgather	formerly	forward
forgave	formic	forwarded
forge	formidable	forwarder
forgery	formula	forwardness
forget	formulate	fossil
forgetful	formulated	fossiliferous
forgetfully	formulates	fossilization
forgetfulness	formulation	fossilize
forgivable	forsake	fossilized
forgive	forsaken	foster
forgiven	forsook	fostered
forgiveness	forsooth	fought
forgivingly	forswear	foul

98

foulard	fragility	frazzled
fouler	fragment	freak
foulest	fragmentary	freakish
foully	fragmentation	freckle
foulness	fragrance	freckled
found	fragrant	free
foundation	fragrantly	freeboard
founded	frail	freeborn
founder	frailty	freedom
foundling	frame	freehand
foundry	framed	freely
fount	framework	freeman
fountain	franc	Freemason
fountainhead	franchise	Freemasonry
foursome	frank	freestone
fowl	frankfurter	freeze
fox	frankly	freezer
foxglove	frankness	freight
foxier	frantic	freighter
foxiest	fraternal	French
foxy	fraternally	frenzied
fracas	fraternity	frenzy
fraction	fraternization	frequency
fractional	fraternize	frequent
fractionally	fraternized	frequently
fractionate	fratricide	fresco
fractionation	fraud	fresh
fracture	fraudulent	freshen
fractured	fraught	freshened
fragile	fray	freshly
fragilely	frazzle	freshman

99

fret
fretful
fretwork
friability
friable
friar
fricassee
friction
frictional
Friday
fried
friend
friendless
friendlier
friendliest
friendliness
friendly
friendship
frieze
frigate
fright
frighten
frightened
frighteningly
frightful
frightfully
frightfulness
frigid
frigidity
frigidly
frill

fringe
frippery
frisky
fritter
frittered
frivolity
frivolous
frivolously
frizzle
frizzled
frock
frog
frogfish
frolic
from
frond
fronded
front
frontage
frontal
fronted
frontier
frontispiece
frost
frostbite
frosted
frostfish
frostily
frostiness
frostwork
frosty

froth
frothed
frothy
froward
frown
frowned
frowningly
frowzily
frowzy
froze
frozen
fructiferous
frugal
frugality
frugally
fruit
fruiterer
fruitful
fruitfully
fruitfulness
fruition
fruitless
fruitlessly
fruitlessness
fruity
frump
frustrate
frustration
fry
fryer
fuchsia

100

fuddle	functionary	furnishings
fuddled	fund	furniture
fudge	fundamental	furor
fuel	fundamentally	furrier
fueled	funded	furriest
fugacious	funeral	furrow
fugitive	funereal	furrowed
fugue	funereally	furry
fulcrum	fungi	further
fulfill	fungible	furtherance
fulfillment	fungicide	furthermore
full	fungoid	furthermost
fuller	fungus	furthest
fullest	funicular	furtive
fully	funnel	furtively
fulminant	funnier	fury
fulminate	funniest	fuse
fulminated	funny	fused
fulmination	fur	fuselage
fulsome	furbelow	fuses
fumble	furbish	fusibility
fumblingly	furious	fusible
fume	furiously	fusilade
fumed	furl	fusion
fumigate	furled	fuss
fumigated	furlong	fussy
fumigation	furlough	futile
fumigator	furloughed	futilely
fun	furnace	futility
function	furnish	future
functional	furnished	futurity

101

G

gabardine
gable
gadfly
gadolinium
gadroon
gaff
gag
gage
gaiety
gaily
gain
gained
gainer
gainful
gainfully
gainsay
gaiter
galantine
galaxy
gale
galena
gall
gallant
gallantry
gallery
galley
gallium

gallon
gallop
gallows
gallstone
galvanism
galvanization
galvanize
galvanized
gambit
gambler
gamboge
gambol
gambrel
game
gameness
gammon
gamut
gander
gang
ganglia
ganglion
gangplank
gangrene
gangrenous
gangster
gangway
gap

garage
garb
garbage
garble
garden
gardner
gardenia
garish
garland
garlic
garment
garner
garnet
garnish
garnishee
garnisher
garnishment
garniture
garret
garrison
garrulity
garrulous
garter
gas
gaseous
gash
gasket

102

gasoline	gear	genetics
gasp	geared	genial
gastralgia	geisha	geniality
gastric	gelatin	genially
gastritis	gelatinize	genii
gastronomic	gelatinoid	genitive
gate	gelatinous	genius
gatehouse	gem	geniuses
gatekeeper	gemmed	genteel
gatepost	gender	gentian
gateway	genealogical	gentile
gather	genealogist	gentility
gatherer	genealogy	gentle
gatherings	genera	gentleman
gaucherie	general	gentlemen
gaudy	generalissimo	gentleness
gauge	generality	gentler
gauntlet	generalization	gentlest
gauntlets	generalize	gently
gauze	generalized	gentry
gave	generally	genuflect
gavel	generalship	genuflection
gavotte	generate	genuine
gay	generation	genuinely
gayety	generative	genuineness
gayly	generator	genus
gayness	generic	geodetic
gaze	generosity	geography
gazelle	generous	geological
gazette	generously	geology
gazetteer	genesis	geometric

geometry	giant	girded
geranium	gibber	girder
gerent	gibbered	girdle
germ	gibberish	girdled
German	gibbon	girl
germane	gibe	girlhood
germicide	giblets	girlish
germinal	giddiness	girth
germinant	giddy	give
germinate	gift	given
germinated	gifted	giver
germination	gig	gizzard
germinative	gigantic	glacial
gerund	giggle	glad
gerundial	giggled	gladden
gerundive	gild	gladdened
gesso	gilded	glade
Gestalt	gilder	gladiator
gesticulate	gill	gladiatorial
gesture	gill	gladiolus
gestured	gilt	gladly
get	gimbals	gladness
geyser	gimlet	Gladstone
ghastliness	gimlets	glamorous
ghastly	gin	glamour
gherkin	ginger	glance
ghetto	gingerly	glanced
ghost	gingham	gland
ghostliness	gingivitis	glandered
ghostly	giraffe	glanders
ghoul	gird	glandular

104

glare	glittered	glued
glared	global	glum
glaringly	globe	glut
glass	globular	glutted
glassful	globule	glutton
glasshouse	gloom	gluttonous
glassiness	gloomily	gluttonously
glassware	gloominess	gluttony
glassy	gloria	glycerin
glaze	glorification	gnarl
glazed	glorify	gnarled
glazier	glorious	gnash
gleam	glory	gnat
gleamed	gloss	gnathic
glean	glossal	gnaw
gleaner	glossary	gnawed
gleeful	glossily	gneiss
glib	glossiness	gnome
glibly	glossitis	gnomic
glide	glossy	gnomon
glided	glottis	gnu
glider	glove	go
glidingly	glover	goal
glimmer	glow	goat
glimpse	glower	goatfish
glint	glowered	goatherd
glioma	glowingly	gobble
glissando	glowworm	goblet
glisten	glucinum	goblets
glistened	glucose	goblin
glitter	glue	gocart

105

god	goodly	governmental
godchild	good-natured	governor
goddess	goodness	gown
godfather	goose	grab
godhead	gooseberry	grace
godhood	gopher	graceful
godless	Gordian	graceless
godlike	gore	gracious
godliness	gored	graciously
godly	gorge	grackle
godparent	gorgeous	gradation
godsend	gorget	grade
godson	gorilla	graded
goggle	gospel	gradient
goings	gossamer	gradual
goiter	gossip	gradually
gold	got	graduate
golden	Gothic	graduated
goldenrod	gotten	graduation
goldfinch	gouache	graft
goldfish	gouge	grafted
goldsmith	gouged	grafter
golf	goulash	grail
golfer	gourd	grain
gondola	gourmet	grained
gondolier	gout	grammar
gone	govern	grammarian
gong	governable	grammatical
goober	governance	granary
good	governess	grand
good-by	government	grandchild

106

grandee	grasp	graybeard
grandeur	graspingly	grayish
grandfather	grass	grayness
grandiloquence	grasshopper	graze
grandiloquent	grassplot	grazier
grandiose	grate	grease
grandly	grated	greasewood
grandmother	grateful	greasier
grandness	grater	greasiest
grandparent	gratification	greasily
grandsire	gratify	greasiness
grandson	gratingly	great
grange	gratis	greatly
granite	gratitude	greatness
graniverous	gratuitous	greed
grant	gratuity	greedier
granted	gravamen	greediest
granular	grave	greedily
granulate	gravel	greediness
granulated	gravely	greedy
granulation	graven	Greek
granule	graver	green
grape	gravest	greenback
grapeshot	gravestone	greener
graph	gravitate	greenery
graphic	gravitated	greenest
graphical	gravitation	greenhorn
graphics	gravitational	greenhouse
graphite	gravity	greenish
grapnel	gravy	greenness
grapple	gray	greenroom

greenwood   grindstone   grossly

greet   grinned   grossness

greeted   grip   grotesque

greetings   gripe   grotesquely

gregarious   gripper   grotto

gregariously   grisly   grouch

Gregorian   grist   grouchily

grenade   gristle   grouchy

grenadier   grit   ground

grenadine   grittiness   grounded

grew   gritty   groundless

grid   grizzle   groundling

griddle   grizzled   groundwork

gridiron   grizzly   group

grief   groan   groupings

grievance   groaned   grouse

grieve   groaningly   grout

grievous   grocer   grove

grievously   grocery   grovel

grill   grog   groveled

grilled   groin   grow

grim   grommet   grower

grimace   groom   growl

grime   groomed   growled

grimly   groove   grown

grimness   grope   growth

grimy   gropingly   grub

grin   grosgrain   grubbiness

grind   gross   grubby

grinder   grosser   grudge

grindingly   grossest   grudgingly

gruel	guidebook	gumption
gruesome	guided	gumshoe
gruff	guidepost	gumwood
gruffer	guidon	gun
gruffest	guild	gunboat
gruffly	guile	guncotton
grumble	guileful	gunfire
grumpiness	guileless	gunlock
grumpy	guillotine	gunman
grunt	guilt	gunner
grunted	guiltily	gunnery
guarantee	guiltless	gunny
guaranteed	guilty	gunpaper
guarantor	guinea	gunpowder
guaranty	guise	gunrunning
guard	guises	gunshop
guarded	guitar	gunshot
guardian	gulch	gunsmith
guardianship	gulden	gunstock
guardroom	gult	gunwale
guardsman	gull	gurgle
guava	gullet	gush
gubernatorial	gullets	gusher
gudgeon	gullibility	gushingly
guerdon	gullible	gushy
guerrilla	gulp	gusset
guess	gum	gust
guesswork	gumbo	gustatory
guest	gumboil	gustily
guidance	gummosis	gusto
guide	gummy	gusty

109

gutter		guzzler		gyrate	
gutteral		gymkhana		gyration	
gutteralize		gymnasium		gyratory	
gutterally		gymnast		gyrfalcon	
gutteralness		gymnastic		gyro	
guttersnipe		gynecologist		gyrocompass	
guy		gynecology		gyroscope	
guzzle		gypsum		gyrostat	
guzzled		gypsy		gyves	

ℋ

haberdasher	hailstone	halter
haberdashery	hailstorm	haltingly
habiliment	hair	halyard
habit	hairbreadth	ham
habitable	hairbrush	hamlet
habitant	haircut	hamlets
habitat	hairpin	hammer
habitation	hairsplitter	hammered
habitual	hairspring	hammerless
habitually	hairy	hammock
habituate	halberd	hamper
habituated	halcyon	hampered
habitude	hale	hamster
hackle	half	hamstring
hackman	halfway	hand
hackneyed	halfwitted	handball
hacksaw	halibut	handbook
had	halitosis	handcuff
haddock	hall	handed
hafnium	hallow	handful
haft	Halloween	handicap
hag	hallucination	handicraft
haggard	hallucinatory	handier
haggle	hallucinosis	handiest
haggled	halo	handily
hail	halogen	handiness
hailed	halt	handiwork

111

handkerchief	harassment	harmonica
handle	harbinger	harmonious
handled	harbor	harmoniously
handmade	harbored	harmonization
handrail	hard	harmonize
handsome	harden	harmonized
handsomely	hardened	harmony
handspring	hardener	harness
handwriting	harder	harp
handy	hardest	harpist
hang	hardier	harpoon
hangar	hardiest	harpooned
hanged	hardihood	harpsichord
hanger	hardiness	harrier
hangman	hardly	harrow
hanker	hardness	harsh
hankered	hardship	harsher
hansom	hardware	harshest
haphazard	hardy	harshly
hapless	hare	harshness
happen	harebrained	harvest
happened	harelip	harvester
happenings	harem	has
happier	hark	hash
happiest	Harlequin	hashish
happily	harm	hasp
happiness	harmed	hassock
happy	harmful	haste
harangue	harmless	hasten
harangued	harmlessly	hastened
harass	harmonic	hastily

112

hastiness	hawker	headgear
hasty	hawkweed	headily
hat	hawse	headings
hatband	hawser	headland
hatch	hawthorn	headless
hatchery	hay	headlight
hatchet	haycock	headline
hatchment	hayfork	headlock
hatchway	hayloft	headlong
hate	haymow	headmaster
hated	hayrack	headpiece
hateful	hayseed	headquarters
hatefully	haystack	headsman
hatefulness	hazard	headspring
hatred	hazardous	headstone
hatter	hazardously	headstrong
haughtily	haze	headwater
haughty	hazel	headway
haul	hazily	headwork
haulage	haziness	heady
hauled	hazy	heal
haunch	he	healed
haunt	head	healer
haunted	headache	health
hauntingly	headband	healthful
have	headboard	healthfulness
haven	headcheese	healthier
haversack	headdress	healthiest
havoc	header	healthily
Hawaiian	headfirst	healthy
hawk	headforemost	heap

113

hear	heavenly	heinous
heard	heavenward	heir
hearer	heavier	heiress
hearings	heaviest	heirloom
hearken	heavily	helical
hearsay	heaviness	helicoid
hearse	heavy	helicopter
heart	Hebraic	heliotrope
heartache	Hebrew	helium
heartbeat	hecatomb	helix
heartbreak	heckle	helm
heartbroken	heckled	helmet
heartburn	hectic	helmeted
hearten	hectograph	helmsman
heartfelt	hedge	help
hearth	hedgehog	helper
hearthstone	hedgerow	helpful
heartier	hedonism	helpfully
heartiest	heed	helpfulness
heartily	heeded	helpings
heartless	heedfully	helpless
hearty	heedfulness	helplessly
heat	heedless	helplessness
heater	heedlessness	helpmate
heath	heel	hem
heathen	heft	hematite
heathenish	hegemony	hemicycle
heathenism	hegira	hemisphere
heather	heifer	hemlock
heave	height	hemorrhage
heaven	heighten	hemp

114

hemstitch	hereditable	herpes
hence	hereditament	herpetology
henceforth	hereditary	herring
henceforward	heredity	hers
henchman	hereinafter	herself
henequen	hereinbefore	hesitance
henhouse	hereon	hesitancy
hepatalgia	heresy	hesitant
hepatic	heretic	hesitate
hepatica	heretical	hesitated
hepatitis	hereto	hesitatingly
hepatotomy	heretofore	hesitation
heptagon	hereunto	heterodox
heptameter	hereupon	heterogeneity
heptangular	herewith	heterogeneous
herald	heritability	hew
heraldic	heritable	hewed
heraldry	heritably	hexagon
herb	heritage	hexagonal
herbaceous	hermetic	hexameter
herbage	hermetically	hexangular
herbal	hermit	hexapod
herbarium	hermitage	hiatus
herbivorous	hernia	hibernate
Herculean	herniotomy	hibernation
herd	hero	hibiscus
here	heroic	hickory
hereabouts	heroical	hid
hereafter	heroine	hidden
hereby	heroism	hide
hereditability	heron	hideous

115

hideously	hint	hoarser
hierarchy	hinted	hoarsest
hieratic	hinterland	hoax
high	hintingly	hobble
highborn	hippodrome	hobby
highboy	hippopotamus	hobnail
higher	hippopotamuses	hobnob
highest	hire	hobo
highland	hired	hock
highlander	hireling	hockey
highly	hirsute	hod
highness	his	hoe
highroad	hiss	hog
highway	histology	hogback
hike	historian	hogfish
hiker	historic	hoggish
hilarious	historical	hogshead
hilarity	history	hoist
hill	histrionic	hokum
hillier	hit	hold
hilliest	hitch	holder
hilliness	hither	holdings
hillock	hitherto	hole
hillside	hive	holiday
hilt	hoar	holily
him	hoard	holiness
himself	hoarded	holland
hinder	hoarder	hollow
hindered	hoardings	hollowed
hindrance	hoarfrost	hollowness
hinge	hoarse	holly

116

hollyhock	homunculus	hope
holocaust	hone	hopeful
holograph	honest	hopefully
holographic	honestly	hopefulness
holster	honesty	hopeless
holy	honey	hopelessly
holystone	honeybee	hopelessness
homage	honeycomb	hoplite
home	honeydew	hopper
homeless	honeyed	hopscotch
homelike	honeymoon	horde
homeliness	honeysuckle	horizon
homely	honk	horizontal
homeopathic	honor	horizontally
homeopathy	honorable	hormone
homesickness	honorably	horn
homespun	honorarium	hornbook
homestead	honorary	horned
homeward	honored	hornet
homework	hood	hornpipe
homicidal	hooded	horology
homicide	hoodlum	horoscope
homiletics	hoodoo	horrible
homilies	hoodwink	horrid
homily	hoof	horrification
hominy	hook	horrify
homogeneity	hooker	horror
homogeneous	hookup	horse
homogenize	hookworm	horseback
homologous	hoop	horsehair
homonym	Hoosier	horseman

117

horseshoe	hound	hug
horseweed	hounded	huge
horsewhip	hour	Huguenot
horsewoman	hourly	hulk
hortatory	house	hull
horticulture	housed	hulled
hose	housefly	hum
hosier	household	human
hosiery	householder	humane
hospice	housekeeper	humaneness
hospitable	housemaid	humanism
hospital	houseroom	humanitarian
hospitality	housetop	humanity
hospitalization	housewarming	humanization
hospitalize	housewife	humanize
host	housework	humanized
hostage	hovel	humankind
hostel	hover	humanly
hostess	how	humble
hostile	however	humbled
hostilely	howitzer	humbleness
hostility	howl	humbly
hot	howsoever	humbug
hotbed	hub	humdrum
hotel	hubbub	humerus
hotheaded	huckleberry	humid
hothouse	huckster	humidifier
hotly	huddle	humidify
hotness	huddled	humidity
hotter	hue	humidor
hottest	huff	humiliate

118

humiliated	hurtful	hydrometer
humiliation	hurtfully	hydrophobia
humility	hurtfulness	hydroplane
hummed	hurtle	hydroponics
hummock	hurtled	hydrostatics
humor	husband	hydroxide
humored	husbandry	hyena
humorist	hush	hygiene
humorous	hushed	hygienic
humorousness	husk	hygienically
hump	huskily	hymn
humus	huskiness	hymnal
hunch	husky	hyperactive
hundred	hussy	hyperalgia
hundredth	hustings	hyperbola
hunger	hustle	hyperbole
hungered	hustled	hypercritical
hungrily	hustler	hyperemia
hungry	hutch	hyperopia
hunk	hyacinth	hypertension
hunt	hyaloid	hyperthyroid
hunted	hybrid	hypertrophy
hunter	hydrangea	hyphen
huntsman	hydrant	hyphenate
hurdle	hydrate	hyphenated
hurdled	hydraulic	hypnosis
hurl	hydrocarbon	hypnotism
hurled	hydrochloric	hypnotist
hurricane	hydrocyanic	hypnotize
hurry	hydroelectric	hypochlorite
hurt	hydrogen	hypochondria

119

hypochondriac	hypotenuse	hypothetical
hypocrisy	hypothecate	hypothetically
hypocrite	hypotheses	hysteria
hypocritical	hypothesis	hysterical
hypodermic	hypothesize	hysterics
hypoglottis	hypothetic	hysteroid

I

iambic	identify	ignominy
Iberian	identity	ignoramus
ibex	idiocy	ignorance
ibis	idiom	ignorant
ice	idiomatic	ignorantly
iceberg	idiosyncrasy	ignore
icebound	idiot	iguana
icehouse	idiotic	ilex
iceman	idle	Iliad
ichneumon	idled	ilk
ichor	idleness	ill
ichthyology	idler	illegal
icicle	idly	illegality
icily	idol	illegibility
iciness	idolater	illegible
icy	idolatrous	illegitimacy
icon	idolatry	illegitimate
idea	idolize	illiberal
ideal	idyl	illicit
idealism	idyllic	illimitable
idealist	if	illinium
idealistic	igloo	illiteracy
idealization	igneous	illiterate
idealize	ignite	illness
ideally	ignition	illogical
identical	ignoble	illuminant
identification	ignominious	illuminate

121

illumination	immaculately	immorally
illuminator	immanent	immortal
illumine	immaterial	immortality
illusion	immature	immortalize
illusive	immaturely	immortally
illusory	immaturity	immovability
illustrate	immeasurable	immovable
illustrated	immediacy	immovableness
illustration	immediate	immovably
illustrative	immediately	immune
illustrator	immediateness	immunity
illustrious	immemorial	immunization
image	immense	immunize
imagery	immensely	immunology
imaginable	immensity	immure
imaginary	immerse	immutability
imagination	immersion	immutable
imaginative	immigrant	imp
imagine	immigration	impact
imaginings	imminence	impaction
imbecile	imminent	impair
imbecility	immobile	impaired
imbibe	immobility	impairment
imbroglio	immobilization	impale
imbue	immobilize	impaled
imitable	immoderate	impalement
imitate	immodest	impalpability
imitation	immolate	impalpable
imitative	immolation	impalpably
imitator	immoral	impanel
immaculate	immorality	impaneled

122

impart	impenetrability	implement
imparted	impenetrable	implicate
impartial	imperative	implication
impartiality	imperceptible	implicit
impartially	imperfect	implicitly
impassability	imperfection	imploration
impasse	imperial	implore
impassible	imperious	imploringly
impassion	imperishable	implied
impassioned	impersonal	imply
impassive	impersonate	impolite
impassively	impertinence	impolitely
impassivity	impertinent	impoliteness
impatience	imperturbable	impolitic
impatient	impervious	imponderable
impeach	impetigo	import
impeachable	impetuosity	importance
impeachment	impetuous	important
impeccability	impetuously	importation
impeccable	impetuousness	importer
impeccant	impetus	importunity
impeccancy	impiety	impose
impecuniosity	impinge	imposingly
impecunious	impingement	imposition
impedance	impious	impossibility
impede	impiously	impossible
impediment	impish	impost
impedimenta	implacability	impostor
impel	implacable	imposture
impelled	implant	impotence
impend	implausible	impotent

123

impound	improvable	inaccurate
impoverish	improve	inaction
impoverishment	improvement	inactive
impower	improvidence	inactivity
impracticability	improvident	inadequacy
impracticable	improvisation	inadequate
imprecate	improvise	inadmissibility
imprecation	imprudence	inadmissible
imprecatory	imprudently	inadvertence
impregnability	impudence	inadvertent
impregnable	impudent	inadvisability
impregnate	impudently	inadvisable
impregnation	impugn	inalienable
impresario	impugnable	inane
imprescriptible	impugned	inanimate
impress	impugnment	inanition
impression	impulse	inanity
impressionable	impulsion	inapplicable
impressionism	impulsive	inapposite
impressionistic	impunity	inappreciable
impressive	impure	inappreciative
imprimatur	impurely	inappropriate
imprint	impurity	inapt
imprison	imputable	inaptitude
imprisoned	imputation	inarticulate
imprisonment	imputative	inartistic
improbability	impute	inasmuch
improbably	inability	inattention
impromptu	inaccessibility	inattentive
improper	inaccessible	inaudibility
impropriety	inaccuracy	inaudible

inaudibly	inchworm	inclusively
inaugural	incidence	incognito
inaugurate	incident	incoherence
inauguration	incidental	incoherent
inauspicious	incidentally	incombustibility
inborn	incinerate	incombustible
inbred	incinerated	income
incalculable	incineration	incommensurable
incandesce	incinerator	incommensurate
incandescence	incipient	incomparable
incandescent	incise	incompatibility
incantation	incised	incompatible
incapable	incision	incompetence
incapacitate	incisive	incompetent
incapacitation	incisively	incomplete
incarcerate	incisiveness	incomprehensi-bility
incarceration	incisor	incomprehensible
incarnate	incitation	incompressi-bility
incarnation	incite	incompressible
incendiarism	incitement	inconceivability
incendiary	incivility	inconceivable
incense	inclemency	inconclusive
incentive	inclement	inconclusiveness
inception	inclination	incongruity
incertitude	incline	incongruous
incessant	inclined	inconsequential
incessantly	inclose	inconsiderable
incest	inclosure	inconsiderate
incestuous	include	inconsiderately
inch	included	inconsistency
inchoate	inclusive	inconsistent

inconsolable	incrustation	indefiniteness
inconspicuous	incubate	indelibility
inconstancy	incubation	indelible
inconstant	incubator	indelicacy
incontestable	incubus	indelicate
incontinence	inculcate	indelicately
incontinent	inculcation	indemnification
incontrovertible	inculpate	indemnify
inconvenience	inculpation	indemnity
inconvenient	inculpatory	indent
inconveniently	incumbency	indentation
inconvertibility	incumbent	indented
inconvertible	incunabula	indention
incorporate	incur	indenture
incorporation	incurable	independence
incorporator	incurably	independent
incorrect	incurred	indescribable
incorrigibility	incursion	indestructible
incorrigible	indebtedness	indeterminable
incorruptibility	indecency	indeterminate
incorruptible	indecent	index
increase	indecently	indexed
increasingly	indecision	indexer
incredibility	indecisive	indexes
incredible	indecorous	Indian
incredulity	indecorum	indicate
incredulous	indeed	indication
increment	indefatigable	indicative
incriminate	indefensible	indicator
incrimination	indefinable	indicatory
incriminatory	indefinite	indices

126

indicia	indistinct	inductive
indict	indistinctly	inductor
indictable	indistinguishable	indulge
indictment	indite	indulgence
indifference	indium	indulgent
indifferent	individual	indurate
indifferently	individualism	industrial
indigence	individualist	industrialism
indigenous	individualistic	industrialist
indigent	individuality	industrialization
indigestibility	individualize	industrialize
indigestible	individually	industrially
indignant	indivisibility	industrious
indignantly	indivisible	industriousness
indignation	indoctrinate	industry
indignity	indoctrination	inebriate
indigo	indolence	inebriation
indirect	indolent	inebriety
indirection	indomitable	inedible
indirectly	indoors	ineffable
indirectness	indorse	ineffably
indiscreet	indorsee	ineffective
indiscretion	indorsement	ineffectual
indiscriminate	indorser	ineffectually
indispensability	indubitable	inefficacious
indispensable	induce	inefficiency
indispose	inducement	inefficient
indisposed	induct	inefficiently
indisposition	inductance	inelastic
indisputable	inducted	inelasticity
indissoluble	induction	inelegance

127

inelegant	inexpedient	infelicity
ineligibility	inexpensive	infer
ineligible	inexperience	inference
ineluctable	inexperienced	inferential
inept	inexpert	inferior
ineptitude	inexplicable	inferiority
inequality	inexplicably	infernal
inequitable	inextricable	infernally
inequity	infallibility	inferno
ineradicable	infallible	inferred
ineradicably	infamous	infertile
inerrancy	infamy	infertility
inerrant	infancy	infest
inert	infant	infestation
inertia	infanticide	infidel
inertly	infantile	infidelity
inertness	infantilism	infield
inessential	infantry	infielder
inestimable	infarct	infiltrate
inestimably	infarction	infiltration
inevitability	infatuate	infinite
inevitable	infatuated	infinitesimal
inevitably	infatuation	infinitesimally
inexact	infeasible	infinitive
inexactitude	infect	infinitude
inexcusable	infected	infinity
inexhaustible	infection	infirm
inexhaustibly	infectious	infirmary
inexorable	infectiously	infirmity
inexpedience	infectiousness	inflame
inexpediency	infelicitous	inflamed

inflammability	infrequent	inhabitance
inflammable	infrequently	inhabitancy
inflammably	infringe	inhabitation
inflammation	infringed	inhabited
inflammatory	infringement	inhalation
inflate	infuriate	inhale
inflated	infuriated	inhaled
inflation	infuse	inhaler
inflationary	infused	inharmonious
inflect	infuses	inhere
inflection	infusion	inhered
inflexibility	ingenious	inherence
inflexible	ingeniously	inherent
inflict	ingenuity	inherently
infliction	ingenuous	inherit
influence	ingest	inheritable
influential	ingestion	inheritance
influenza	inglorious	inherited
influx	ingot	inheritor
inform	ingrain	inhibit
informal	ingrained	inhibited
informality	ingratiate	inhibition
informant	ingratiated	inhibitory
information	ingratiation	inhospitable
informative	ingratiatory	inhospitably
informed	ingratitude	inhuman
informer	ingredient	inhumane
informingly	ingress	inhumanity
infraction	ingrown	inimical
infrangible	inhabit	inimitable
infrared	inhabitable	inimitably

iniquitous	inkwell	inoculation
iniquitously	inky	inoffensive
iniquity	inlaid	inoperable
initial	inland	inoperative
initialed	inlay	inopportune
initially	inlet	inordinate
initiate	inlets	inorganic
initiated	inmate	inpatient
initiation	inmost	inquest
initiative	inn	inquietude
initiator	innate	inquire
initiatory	innately	inquired
inject	inner	inquirer
injected	innermost	inquires
injection	inning	inquiries
injector	innings	inquiringly
injudicious	innkeeper	inquiry
injudiciously	innocence	inquisition
injunction	innocent	inquisitive
injure	innocently	inquisitor
injured	innocuous	inquisitorial
injurious	innocuously	inroad
injury	innovate	insane
injustice	innovation	insanely
injustices	innovative	insanitary
ink	innovator	insanitation
inked	innuendo	insanity
inkhorn	innumerable	insatiability
inkling	inobservant	insatiable
inklings	inoculate	inscribe
inkstand	inoculated	inscriber

130

inscription	insignificant	inspiration
inscrutability	insincere	inspirational
inscrutable	insincerely	inspiratory
insect	insincerity	inspire
insecticide	insinuate	inspired
insectivorous	insinuated	inspirer
insecure	insinuatingly	inspiringly
insecurity	insinuation	inspiritingly
insensate	insipid	instability
insensibility	insipidity	install
insensible	insipidly	installation
insensitive	insist	installed
insensitiveness	insisted	installment
insentience	insistence	instance
insentient	insistent	instant
inseparable	insobriety	instantaneous
inseparably	insole	instanter
insert	insolence	instantly
inserted	insolent	instate
insertion	insolently	instead
inset	insolubility	instep
inshore	insoluble	instigate
inside	insolvable	instigated
insider	insolvency	instigation
insides	insolvent	instigator
insidious	insomnia	instill
insidiously	insomuch	instilled
insight	insouciance	instinct
insigne	inspect	instinctive
insignia	inspection	instinctively
insignificance	inspector	institute

131

instituted	insuppressible	intelligent
institution	insurability	intelligibility
institutional	insurable	intelligible
instruct	insurance	intemperance
instruction	insure	intemperate
instructional	insured	intemperately
instructive	insurer	intend
instructor	insurgency	intendant
instrument	insurgent	intended
instrumental	insurmountable	intense
instrumentalist	insurrection	intensification
instrumentality	insurrectionary	intensifier
instrumentally	insurrectionist	intensify
instrumentation	intact	intensity
insubordinate	intaglio	intensive
insubordination	intake	intent
insufferable	intangibility	intention
insufficiency	intangible	intentional
insufficient	integer	intentionally
insular	integral	intently
insularity	integrally	intentness
insulate	integrate	interact
insulated	integrated	interaction
insulation	integration	interborough
insulator	integrity	interbreed
insulin	integument	intercede
insult	intellect	interceded
insulted	intellectual	intercept
insultingly	intellectualize	intercepted
insuperable	intellectually	interception
insupportable	intelligence	interceptor

132

intercession

intercessory

interchange

interchangeability

interchangeable

intercollegiate

intercommunicate

interconnect

intercostal

intercourse

interde-
nominational

interdependent

interdependence

interdict

interdiction

interest

interested

interestedly

interestingly

interfere

interfered

interference

interferingly

interim

interior

interject

interjection

interlace

interlaced

interlard

interleaf

interleave

interline

interlineal

interlinear

interlineation

interlined

interlobar

interlock

interlocked

interlocutor

interlocutory

interloper

interlude

intermarriage

intermarry

intermediary

intermediate

interment

intermezzo

interminable

interminably

intermingle

intermingled

intermission

intermit

intermittence

intermittent

intermittently

intermixture

intern

internal

internally

international

internationalize

internationally

interne

internecine

internment

interpellate

interpellation

interplanetary

interpolate

interpolated

interpolation

interpose

interposition

interpret

interpretation

interpretative

interpreted

interpreter

interregnum

interrelation

interrogate

interrogation

interrogative

interrogatory

interrupt

interruptedly

interruption

interscapular

interscholastic

intersect	intolerable	introductory
intersperse	intolerance	introit
interstate	intolerant	introspect
interstellar	intonation	introspection
interstice	intone	introspective
interstices	intoned	introversion
interstitial	intoxicant	introvert
interstitially	intoxicate	intrude
intertwine	intoxicated	intruded
interval	intoxication	intruder
intervene	intractability	intrusion
intervened	intractable	intrusive
intervention	intramural	intrusively
interview	intransigence	intuition
interviewed	intransigent	intuitive
interviewer	intransitive	intuitively
interweave	intrastate	inunction
interwoven	intrenchment	inundate
intestacy	intrepid	inundated
intestate	intrepidity	inundation
intestinal	intrepidly	inure
intestine	intricacies	invade
intimacy	intricacy	invaded
intimate	intricate	invalid
intimated	intricately	invalidate
intimately	intrigue	invalidated
intimation	intrigued	invalidation
intimidate	intrinsic	invalidity
intimidated	introduce	invaluable
intimidation	introduced	invar
into	introduction	invariability

invariable	invidious	inwardness
invariableness	invidiously	iodate
invasion	invigorate	iodic
invective	invigorated	iodide
inveigh	invigoration	iodine
inveigle	invincibility	iodize
inveigled	invincible	ion
invent	inviolability	Ionic
invention	inviolable	ionization
inventive	inviolate	ionize
inventively	invisibility	iota
inventiveness	invisible	ipecac
inventor	invitation	Iranian
inventory	invite	irascibility
inverse	invited	irascible
inversion	invitingly	irate
invert	invocation	irately
inverted	invoice	iridectomy
invertible	invoices	iridescence
invest	invoke	iridescent
invested	invoked	iridium
investigate	involuntarily	iris
investigated	involuntary	Irish
investigation	involute	Irishman
investigative	involution	iritis
investigator	involve	irk
investiture	involved	irksome
investment	invulnerability	iron
investor	invulnerable	ironclad
invests	inward	ironed
inveterate	inwardly	ironical

135

ironside	irresolute	isolation
ironware	irresolution	isolationist
ironwood	irrespective	isomer
ironwork	irresponsibility	isomeric
irony	irresponsible	isotherm
Iroquois	irretraceable	issuance
irradiate	irretrievable	issue
irradiated	irreverence	issued
irradiation	irreverent	issues
irrational	irreversible	isthmus
irrationally	irrevocable	it
irreconcilability	irrigable	Italian
irreconcilable	irrigate	Italianate
irrecoverable	irrigated	italic
irredeemable	irrigation	italicize
irreducible	irritability	itch
irrefragable	irritable	itchier
irrefrangible	irritant	itchiest
irrefutable	irritate	itchy
irregular	irritated	item
irregularity	irritation	itemize
irrelevance	irritative	itemized
irrelevant	irruption	iterate
irreligious	ischium	itineracy
irremediable	isinglass	itinerancy
irremovable	Islam	itinerant
irreparable	island	itinerary
irreplaceable	islander	itinerate
irrepressible	isle	its
irreproachable	isobar	itself
irresistible	isolate	ivory

136

J

jabber

jabot

jack

jackal

jackanapes

jackdaw

jacket

jackknife

jackstraw

Jacobean

jade

jadeite

jaguar

jail

jailed

jailer

jam

jamboree

jammed

jangle

janitor

janitress

January

japan

Japanese

jar

jargon

jarred

jasmine

jasper

jaundice

jaunt

jauntier

jauntiest

jauntily

jauntiness

jaunty

javelin

jawbone

jealous

jealousy

jeer

jeeringly

Jehovah

jejune

jellied

jelly

jellyfish

jeopardize

jeopardy

jeremiad

jerk

jerkily

jerky

jersey

jest

jester

jestingly

Jesuit

Jesus

jet

jetsam

jettison

jetty

jewel

jeweled

jeweler

jewelry

Jewish

Jewry

jibe

jig

jigger

jiggle

jiggled

jigsaw

jingle

jingled

jingo

jingoism

jinrikisha

jinx	jolly	judicative
jitney	jonquil	judicatory
job	jostle	judicature
jobber	jostled	judicial
jockey	jot	judicially
jocose	jounce	judiciary
jocosely	journal	judicious
jocosity	journalism	juggle
jocular	journalist	juggled
jocularity	journalize	juggler
jocularly	journey	jugular
jocund	journeyed	juice
jocundity	jovial	juicy
jog	joviality	julep
jogged	jovially	July
joggle	jowl	jumble
join	joy	jumbo
joinder	joyful	jump
joined	joyfully	jumper
joiner	joyfulness	junction
joinings	joyless	juncture
joint	joyous	June
jointed	jubilance	jungle
jointly	jubilant	junior
jointure	jubilate	juniper
joist	jubilation	junk
joke	jubilee	junket
joker	judge	jurat
jokingly	judged	juridical
jollification	judgeship	jurisconsult
jollity	judgment	jurisdiction

138

jurisprudence
jurist
juror
jury
juryman
just

justice
justifiable
justification
justificatory
justified
justify

justly
justness
jute
juvenile
juvenility
juxtaposition

K

kaiser

kale

kaleidoscope

kaleidoscopic

kangaroo

kaolin

kapok

karma

kava

kayak

keel

keen

keenly

keenness

keep

keeper

keg

kelp

kennel

kept

keratin

kerchief

kernel

kerosene

kersey

kestrel

ketch

140

ketosis

kettle

key

keyboard

keyed

khaki

khedive

kibitzer

kick

kicker

kid

kidnap

kidnaped

kidney

kilerg

kill

killed

killer

killings

kiln

kilocycle

kilogram

kilometer

kilt

kilted

kin

kind

kinder

kindest

kindle

kindled

kindliness

kindly

kindness

kindred

kine

kinesthetic

kinetic

king

kingbird

kingbolt

kingcraft

kingdom

kingfish

kingfisher

kinglet

kinglets

kingliness

kingly

kingpin

kingship

kink

kinship

kinsman

kiosk	knifed	knowable
kipper	knight	knowingly
kitchen	knighted	knowingness
kitchenette	knighthood	knowledge
kite	knightliness	known
kith	knightly	knuckle
kitten	knights	knuckled
kleptomania	knit	knurl
kleptomaniac	knitter	knurled
klieg	knives	knurly
knapsack	knob	kobold
knave	knock	kodak
knavery	knockdown	kohlrabi
knavish	knocker	kopeck
kneecap	knockout	Koran
kneel	knoll	kosher
kneeled	knot	kraft
knelt	knothole	kremlin
knew	knotted	kulak
knickers	knotty	krypton
knickknack	knout	kymograph
knife	know	kyphosis

L

label	lactation	lamed
labeled	lacteal	lamely
labial	lactic	lameness
labor	lactose	lament
laboratory	lacuna	lamentable
labored	lacunae	lamentation
laborer	ladder	lamented
laborious	laden	lamina
laboriously	ladle	laminate
laburnum	ladled	laminated
labyrinth	lady	lamination
lace	ladylike	lampoon
laced	ladyship	lamprey
lacerate	lag	lance
lacerated	laggard	lancer
laceration	lagged	lancet
laches	lagoon	lancinating
lachrymal	lair	lancination
lachrymose	laird	land
lacings	laity	landau
lack	lake	landed
lackey	lambdoid	landfall
laconic	lambent	landholder
lacquer	lambkin	landlady
lacquered	lamblike	landlocked
lacrosse	lambrequin	landlord
lactate	lame	landmark

142

landscape	larger	lately
landslip	largess	latency
landsman	largest	lateness
landward	lariat	latent
language	lark	later
languid	larkspur	lateral
languish	larva	laterally
languishingly	larvae	latest
languor	larval	lath
languorous	laryngeal	lather
lanky	laryngitis	laths
lanolin	larynx	Latin
lansdowne	lascar	Latinism
lantern	lascivious	Latinity
lanthanum	lash	latitude
lanyard	lashed	latitudinal
lap	lashings	latitudinarian
lapel	lassitude	latter
lapful	lasso	lattermost
lapidary	last	lattice
lapse	lasted	latticework
lapsed	lastingly	laud
lapwing	lastly	laudability
larboard	lasts	laudable
larcenous	Latakia	laudanum
larceny	latch	laudation
larch	latched	laudatory
lard	latchkey	laugh
large	latchstring	laughable
largely	late	laughingly
largeness	lateen	laughingstock

143

laughter	layer	leased
launch	layman	leasehold
launchings	lazaretto	leaseholder
launder	lazier	leash
laundered	laziest	least
laundress	lazily	leather
laundry	laziness	leatheret
laundryman	lazy	leathern
laureate	leach	leatheroid
laurel	lead	leathery
lava	leaden	leave
lavalliere	leader	leaven
lavatory	leadership	leavings
lavender	leadsman	lecithin
lavish	leaf	lectern
law	leaflet	lecture
lawbreaker	leaflets	lectured
lawful	league	lecturer
lawfully	leagued	ledger
lawgiver	leak	leech
lawless	leakage	leek
lawlessness	leakiness	leer
lawmaker	leaky	leered
lawn	lean	leeringly
lawsuit	leaned	leeward
lawyer	leanings	leeway
lax	leap	left
laxative	learn	left-handed
laxity	learned	leg
laxly	learnt	legacy
laxness	lease	legal

144

legalism	leguminous	leper
legalistic	leisure	leprosy
legality	leisureliness	leprous
legalization	leisurely	lesion
legalize	lemon	less
legally	lemonade	lessee
legate	lemur	lessen
legatee	lend	lessened
legation	length	lesser
legato	lengthen	lesson
legend	lengthened	lest
legendary	lengthily	let
legerdemain	lengthiness	lethal
leggings	lengthways	lethargic
legibility	lengthwise	lethargical
legible	lengthy	lethargy
legion	lenience	lets
legionary	leniency	letter
legislate	lenient	lettered
legislation	leniently	letterhead
legislative	lenitive	letterpress
legislator	lenity	letters
legislature	lens	lettuce
legitimacy	Lent	leucocyte
legitimate	Lenten	leucocytosis
legitimately	lenticular	leucoderma
legitimateness	lentigo	leukemia
legitimation	lentil	levant
legitimatize	lentoid	levee
legitimist	leonine	level
legume	leopard	leveled

145

leveler	librarian	ligature
lever	library	ligatured
leverage	libretto	light
levitate	lice	lighted
levitation	license	lighten
levity	licensee	lightened
levulose	licentiate	lighter
levy	licentious	lighterage
lexicography	licentiousness	lightest
lexicon	lichen	lightheaded
liability	licit	lighthouse
liable	lick	lightly
liana	licorice	lightness
liar	lictor	lightning
libation	lie	lightship
libel	liege	lightweight
libeled	lien	ligneous
libelant	lieu	lignify
libelee	lieutenancy	lignite
libeler	lieutenant	likable
libelous	life	like
liberal	lifeguard	liked
liberalism	lifeless	likelihood
liberality	lifelike	likely
liberalization	lifelong	liken
liberalize	lifetime	likeness
liberally	lifework	likewise
liberate	lift	likings
liberation	ligament	lilac
liberator	ligate	liliaceous
liberty	ligation	lilt

146

liltingly	lineament	liquefy
lily	linear	liquescence
limb	lineman	liquescent
limber	linen	liquid
limbo	liner	liquidate
lime	linger	liquidated
limekiln	lingered	liquidation
limelight	lingerie	liquidator
limen	lingo	liquor
Limerick	lingual	lira
limestone	linguist	lisp
limewater	linguistic	lispingly
liminal	linguistically	lissome
limit	linguistics	list
limitable	liniment	listed
limitation	linings	listen
limited	link	listened
limitless	linkage	listener
limnology	linnet	listings
limousine	linoleum	listless
limp	linotype	litany
limpet	linseed	liter
limpid	lint	literacy
limpidity	lintel	literal
limpidly	lion	literalism
limply	lioness	literality
limpness	lionize	literalize
linden	lipoid	literally
line	lipoma	literary
lineage	liquefaction	literate
lineal	liquefiable	literature

litharge	livelong	localize
lithe	lively	locally
lithesome	liver	locate
lithia	livery	location
lithium	livid	loci
lithographer	livings	lock
lithographic	lizard	lockage
lithography	llama	locker
lithosis	llano	locket
lithotomy	load	lockjaw
Lithuania	loaded	lockout
litigable	loadings	locksmith
litigant	loaf	lockup
litigate	loafer	locomotion
litigation	loam	locomotive
litigious	loan	locus
litmus	loaned	locust
litter	loathe	locution
littered	loathed	lode
little	loathful	lodestar
littlest	loathly	lodge
littoral	loathsome	lodger
liturgical	loaves	lodgings
liturgy	lobar	lodgment
livable	lobby	loft
live	lobbyist	loftily
live	lobster	loftiness
lived	local	lofty
liveliest	localism	log
livelihood	locality	loganberry
liveliness	localization	logarithm

148

loggia	longitudinal	lose
logic	longshoreman	loses
logical	look	losings
logician	lookout	loss
logistics	loom	lost
logotype	loomed	lotion
logwood	loon	lottery
loin	loony	lotus
loiter	loop	loud
loitered	loophole	louder
loiterer	loose	loudest
loll	loosely	loudly
lolled	loosen	loudness
lollipop	loosened	lounge
lone	looseness	louse
loneliness	looser	lout
lonely	loosest	loutish
lonesome	loot	louver
lonesomely	lop	lovable
lonesomeness	lopsided	love
long	loquacious	loveless
longboat	loquaciously	loveliness
longed	loquacity	lovelorn
longer	lord	lovely
longest	lordliness	lover
longevity	lordly	lovesick
longhand	lordosis	lovingly
longhorn	lordship	low
longingly	lore	lowborn
longings	lorgnette	lowboy
longitude	losable	lowbred

lower	lug	lurk
lowermost	luggage	luscious
lowest	lugger	lush
lowland	lugubrious	lust
lowliness	lukewarm	luster
lowly	lull	lustful
lowness	lullaby	lustily
loyal	lulled	lustiness
loyalist	lumbago	lustrous
loyally	lumber	lustrously
loyalty	luminary	lustrum
lozenge	luminescent	lusty
lubricant	luminiferous	lute
lubricate	luminosity	luxuriance
lubrication	luminous	luxuriant
lubricator	lump	luxuriate
lucent	lumpy	luxurious
lucid	lunacy	luxury
lucidity	lunar	lyceum
lucidly	lunatic	lyddite
luck	lunch	lymph
luckily	luncheon	lymphatic
luckiness	lunette	lymphoid
luckless	lung	lynx
lucky	lunge	lyonnaise
lucrative	lurch	lyre
lucre	lurched	lyric
lucubration	lure	lyrical
ludicrous	lurid	lyricism

M

macabre	madness	magnificence
macadam	madrigal	magnificent
macadamize	maffia	magnifico
macaroni	magazine	magnifier
macaroon	magenta	magnify
macaw	maggot	magniloquent
macerate	Magi	magnitude
maceration	magic	magnolia
Mach	magical	magnum
machete	magician	magpie
machicolation	magisterial	maguey
machinate	magistracy	maharajah
machination	magistral	mahatma
machine	magistrate	mahogany
machined	magistrature	maid
machinery	magnanimous	maiden
machinist	magnate	maidenhair
mackerel	magnesia	maidenhood
macrocosm	magnesium	maidenly
macron	magnet	maidservant
maculate	magnetic	mail
madam	magnetically	mailability
madder	magnetism	mailable
maddest	magnetization	mailed
madhouse	magnetize	mailer
madly	magneto	mailings
madman	magnification	maim

maimed

main

mainland

mainly

mainmast

mainsail

mainsheet

mainspring

mainstay

maintain

maintainable

maintenance

majestic

majesty

majolica

major

majored

majority

majuscule

make

make-believe

maker

makeshift

makings

malachite

maladjustment

maladminister

maladroit

malady

malapert

malapropos

malaria

malarial

malassimilation

Malay

malcontent

male

malediction

maledictory

malefactor

maleficence

maleficent

malevolence

malevolent

malfeasance

malformed

malice

malicious

maliciously

maliciousness

malign

malignancy

malignant

malignantly

maligned

malignity

malignly

malinger

malingerer

mallard

malleability

malleable

malleolar

malleolus

mallet

malmsey

malnutrition

malodorous

malposition

malpractice

malt

Maltese

maltose

maltreat

malversation

mammal

mammon

mammoth

man

manacle

manage

manageability

manageable

manageably

management

manager

managerial

managerially

managership

manatee

mandamus

mandarin

mandate

mandated	manifold	mantis
mandatory	manifolder	mantle
mandible	manikin	manual
mandibular	manipulate	manually
mandolin	manipulated	manufactory
mandrake	manipulates	manufacture
mandrel	manipulation	manufactured
maneuver	manipulative	manufacturer
maneuvered	manipulator	manumission
manganate	manipulatory	manure
manganese	mankind	manuscript
manger	manlike	Manx
mangily	manliness	many
manginess	manly	map
mangle	manna	maple
mangled	manner	mapped
mango	mannered	mar
mangrove	mannerism	marabou
mangy	mannerly	maraschino
manhole	mannish	maraud
manhood	manometer	marauder
mania	manometric	marble
maniac	manor	March
maniacal	manorial	marcher
manicure	mansard	marchioness
manicurist	manservant	marconigram
manifest	mansion	mare
manifestation	manslaughter	margarine
manifestly	manteau	margin
manifesto	mantel	marginal
manifests	mantilla	marginalia

marginally	marred	mashed
margrave	marriage	masher
marigold	marriageable	mashie
marinate	married	mask
marinated	marrow	masked
marination	marrowbone	masker
marine	marrowfat	mason
mariner	marrowy	masonic
marionette	marry	masonry
Marist	Mars	masquerade
marital	marshal	mass
maritime	marshaled	massacre
marjoram	marshiness	massage
mark	marshmallow	massive
marked	marshy	mast
markedly	marsupial	master
marker	mart	mastered
market	marten	masterful
marketability	martial	masterfully
marketable	martially	masterfulness
markings	martinet	masterly
marksman	martyr	masterpiece
marl	martyrdom	mastership
marlin	marvel	masterwork
marmalade	marveled	mastery
marmoset	marvelous	masthead
marmot	mascara	mastic
maroon	mascot	masticate
marooned	masculine	mastication
marplot	masculinity	masticatory
marquisette	mash	mastiff

154

mastodon	matriculates	May
mastoid	matriculation	mayhem
mastoiditis	matrimonial	mayonnaise
mat	matrimonially	mayor
matador	matrimony	mayoralty
match	matrix	mazurka
matchless	matron	meadow
matchlessly	matronly	meager
matchmaker	matter	meal
matchwood	mattock	mealtime
material	mattress	mean
materialism	maturation	meander
materialist	mature	meaningless
materialistic	matured	meaningly
materiality	maturely	meanings
materialization	matureness	meanly
materialize	maturity	meanness
materialized	matutinal	meantime
materially	maudlin	meanwhile
maternal	maul	measles
maternally	mauled	measurable
maternity	mausoleum	measurably
mathematician	mauve	measure
mathematics	maverick	measured
matinee	mavis	measureless
matriarch	mawkish	measurement
matriarchy	maxillary	measurer
matrices	maxim	meat
matricide	maximal	meatus
matriculate	maximize	mechanic
matriculated	maximum	mechanical

mechanically	medieval	melodiously
mechanician	medievally	melodrama
mechanics	mediocre	melodramatic
mechanism	mediocrity	melody
mechanization	meditate	melon
mechanize	meditated	melt
medal	meditation	meltable
medalist	meditative	melted
medalists	medium	meltingly
medallion	mediums	member
meddle	medlar	membership
meddled	meek	membrane
meddler	meekly	membranous
meddlesome	meekness	memento
media	meerschaum	memoir
medial	meet	memorabilia
median	meetings	memorable
mediate	megacycle	memoranda
mediated	megaphone	memorandum
mediation	meiosis	memorandums
mediative	melancholia	memorial
mediator	melancholic	memorization
medical	melancholy	memorize
medically	melanosis	memory
medicament	meliorate	menace
medicate	melioration	menage
medication	mellifluous	menagerie
medicative	mellow	mend
medicinal	melodeon	mendacious
medicinally	melodic	mendacity
medicine	melodious	mended

156

mendicancy	interest	metalloid
mendicant	meretricious	metallurgic
menhaden	merge	metallurgical
menial	merger	metallurgy
menially	meridian	metamorphose
meningitis	meringue	metamorphosis
mensuration	merino	metaphor
mensurative	merit	metaphorical
mental	merited	metaphysical
mentality	meritorious	metaphysician
mentally	meritoriously	metaphysics
menthol	mermaid	metastasis
mention	merrily	metatarsus
mentioned	merriment	meteor
mentor	merry	meteoric
menu	merrymaking	meteorite
mephitic	mesa	meteoroid
mercantile	mescal	meteorology
mercenary	mesh	meter
mercerize	mesmerism	methane
merchandise	mesmerize	method
merchant	message	methodical
merchantman	messenger	methodist
merciful	Messiah	methodize
merciless	messmate	methodology
mercilessly	metabolic	methyl
mercurial	metabolism	meticulous
mercury	metacarpal	metonymy
mercy	metacarpus	metric
mere	metal	metrical
merely	metallic	metrology

157

metronome	midmost	miler
metropolis	midnight	milestone
metropolitan	midriff	miliary
mettle	midshipman	militancy
mettlesome	midst	militant
mezzanine	midstream	militarism
miasma	midsummer	militarist
miasmal	midway	militaristic
miasmatic	midweek	military
mica	midwife	militate
micaceous	midwinter	militated
microbe	midyear	militia
microbiology	might	milk
microcephalus	mightily	milkings
microcosm	mightiness	milkman
microfilm	mighty	milkweed
micrometer	migraine	milky
micron	migrate	mill
microorganism	migration	milled
microphone	migratory	millenary
microscope	mikado	millennial
microscopic	milch	millennium
microtome	mild	miller
Midas	milder	milline
middle	mildest	milliner
middleman	mildew	millinery
middleweight	mildly	million
midge	mildness	millionaire
midget	mile	millionth
midiron	mileage	millpond
midland	milepost	millstone

158

millwright	ministerially	misalliance
Miltonic	ministration	misanthrope
mime	ministry	misanthropic
mimeograph	mink	misanthropical
mimetic	minnow	misanthropist
mimic	minor	misanthropy
mimicry	minority	misapplication
mimosa	minster	misapply
minaret	minstrel	misapprehension
minatory	minstrelsy	misappropriate
mince	mint	misappropriation
mincingly	minuend	misarrange
mind	minus	misbegotten
minded	minuscule	misbehave
mindful	minute	misbehavior
mine	minute	miscalculate
miner	minuteness	miscall
mineral	minutia	miscarriage
mineralogy	minutiae	miscarry
mingle	minx	miscegenation
mingled	miracle	miscellanea
miniature	miraculous	miscellaneous
minim	mirage	miscellanist
minimal	mire	miscellany
minimization	mired	mischance
minimize	mirror	mischief
minimum	mirth	mischievous
minion	mirthful	miscible
minister	mirthfully	misconceive
ministered	mirthless	misconception
ministerial	misadventure	misconduct

159

misconstruction	misjudged	misspellings
misconstrue	mislay	misspent
miscount	mislead	misstate
miscreant	misleadingly	misstatement
misdate	mislike	mistake
misdeal	mismade	mistaken
misdeed	mismanage	mistakenly
misdemeanor	mismate	misteach
misdirect	misname	mistiness
misdirection	misnamed	mistletoe
misdoubt	misnomer	mistook
miser	misplace	mistranslate
miserable	misprint	mistranslation
miserliness	misprision	mistreat
miserly	mispronounce	mistreatment
misery	mispronunciation	mistress
misfeasance	misquotation	mistrial
misfire	misquote	mistrust
misfit	misread	mistrustful
misformed	misreadings	misty
misfortune	misremember	misunderstand
misgivings	misrepresent	misunderstood
misgovern	misrepresentation	misuse
misguide	misrule	mite
mishap	miss	miter
misinform	missile	mitered
misinformed	mission	mitigable
misinterpret	missionary	mitigate
misinterpretation	missive	mitigation
misinterpreted	misspell	mitosis
misjudge	misspelled	mitral

160

mitten	modern	moisture
mix	modernism	molar
mixed	modernist	molasses
mixer	modernity	mold
mixture	modernize	molded
mnemonic	modernized	moldy
moan	modest	mole
moaned	modestly	molecular
moat	modesty	molecule
mob	modicum	molehill
mobile	modification	molest
mobility	modified	molestation
mobilization	modifier	molests
mobilize	modify	mollification
mobilized	modish	mollify
moccasin	modishly	mollusk
Mocha	modishness	molt
mock	modulate	molten
mockery	modulated	molybdenum
mockingly	modulates	moment
modal	modulation	momentarily
modality	modulator	momentary
mode	module	momently
model	modulus	momentous
modeled	mohair	momentum
moderate	Mohammedan	monarch
moderated	moiety	monarchial
moderately	moist	monarchism
moderateness	moisten	monarchist
moderation	moistened	monarchistic
moderator	moistener	monarchy

161

monastery	monosyllabic	moorish
monastic	monosyllable	moose
monasticism	monotone	moot
Monday	monotonous	mop
monetary	monotony	moraine
monetization	monotype	moral
monetize	monoxide	morale
money	monsoon	moralist
moneyed	monster	moralistic
mongoose	monstrance	moralists
mongrel	monstrosity	morality
monitor	monstrous	moralization
monitored	month	moralize
monk	monthly	moralized
monkey	monument	morally
monocle	monumental	morass
monody	monumentally	moratorium
monogamous	mood	moray
monogamy	moodily	morbid
monogram	moodiness	morbidity
monograph	moody	morbidly
monolith	moon	mordant
monologue	moonbeam	more
monomania	moonfish	moreover
monoplane	moonlight	morgue
monopolism	moonshine	Mormon
monopolist	moonstone	morning
monopolistic	moonstruck	mornings
monopolization	moor	morocco
monopolize	moored	moron
monopoly	moorings	morose

162

morosely	mother-in-law	mourned
morphine	motherland	mourner
morphinism	motherless	mournful
morphology	motherliness	mouse
morris	motherly	mouser
morsel	mother-of-pearl	mousse
mortal	motif	mouth
mortality	motion	mouthed
mortally	motioned	mouthful
mortar	motionless	mouthpiece
mortgage	motivate	movability
mortgagee	motivation	movable
mortgagor	motive	move
mortification	motley	moved
mortify	motor	movement
mortise	motored	mover
mortmain	motorist	movie
mortuary	motorists	movingly
Moslem	motorman	mow
mosque	mottle	mow
mosquito	mottled	mower
moss	motto	much
mossback	mound	mucilage
mossiness	mount	mucilaginous
mossy	mountain	muck
most	mountaineer	mucoid
mostly	mountainous	mucosa
motet	mountebank	mucous
moth	mounted	mucus
mother	mountings	mud
motherhood	mourn	muddier

163

muddiest	multiple	murdered
muddily	multiplex	murderer
muddiness	multiplicand	murderous
muddle	multiplicate	muriatic
muddled	multiplication	murk
muddy	multiplicative	murkily
mudfish	multiplicity	murkiness
muff	multiplier	murky
muffin	multiply	murmur
muffle	multitude	murmured
muffled	multitudinous	murmurer
muffler	multivalent	murmurous
mufti	mumble	muscadine
mug	mumbled	muscatel
mugginess	mummer	muscle
muggy	mummery	muscular
mulatto	mummification	muscularity
mulberry	mummify	muscularly
mulch	mummy	musculature
mulct	mumps	muse
mulcted	munch	mused
mule	mundane	museum
muleteer	municipal	mush
mullion	municipality	mushroom
multifarious	municipally	mushy
multifold	munificence	music
multiform	munificent	musical
multiformity	muniment	musicale
multigraph	munition	musician
multilith	mural	musicianly
multimillionaire	murder	musk

164

musket	muteness	myeloid
musketeer	mutilate	myoma
musketry	mutilated	myopia
muskmelon	mutilation	myopic
muskrat	mutilator	myosis
muslin	mutineer	myotic
muss	mutinous	myotomy
mussed	mutiny	myriad
mussel	mutter	myrrh
mussy	muttered	myrtle
must	mutterings	myself
mustache	mutton	mysterious
mustang	mutual	mysteriously
mustard	mutuality	mystery
muster	mutually	mystic
mustered	muzzle	mystical
mustiness	muzzled	mysticism
musty	my	mystification
mutability	mycology	mystify
mutable	mycosis	myth
mutate	mydriasis	mythical
mutation	mydriatic	mythological
mutative	myectomy	mythology

N

nacelle

nacre

nacreous

nadir

naiad

nail

nailed

nainsook

naïve

naïvete

naked

namable

name

named

nameless

namelessly

namely

namesake

nankeen

napery

naphtha

napkin

napoleon

Napoleonic

narcissus

narcosis

narcotic

narcotism

narcotize

narrate

narration

narrative

narrator

narrow

narrowed

narrower

narrowest

narrowly

narrowness

narwhal

nasal

nasality

nasalize

nasally

nascent

nastier

nastiest

nastily

nastiness

nasturtium

nasty

natal

natation

natatorium

nation

national

nationalism

nationalistic

nationality

nationalization

nationalize

nationally

native

nativity

natural

naturalism

naturalist

naturalistic

naturalization

naturalize

naturalized

naturally

naturalness

nature

naughtily

naughtiness

naughty

nausea

nauseate

nauseated

nauseous

nautical	necessitous	neglectful
nautilus	necessity	negligence
naval	neck	negligent
navigable	neckband	negligible
navigate	neckcloth	negotiability
navigation	neckerchief	negotiable
navigator	necklace	negotiate
navy	necktie	negotiated
neap	neckwear	negotiation
Neapolitan	necrology	negotiator
near	necromancy	Negro
neared	necropolis	negrophile
nearer	necropsy	neighbor
nearest	necrosis	neighborhood
nearly	nectar	neighborly
nearness	nectarine	neither
nearsighted	need	nematode
neat	needed	Nemesis
neater	needful	neolithic
neatest	needfully	neon
neatly	needier	neophyte
neatness	neediest	neoplasm
nebula	neediness	nepenthe
nebular	needle	nephew
nebulosity	needled	nepotism
nebulous	needless	nephralgia
necessarily	needlework	nephrectomy
necessary	nefarious	nephritis
necessitate	negation	nerve
necessitated	negative	nerveless
necessities	neglect	nervous

167

nescience
nest
nestle
nestled
nether
nettle
nettled
network
neural
neuralgia
neurasthenia
neurasthenic
neurectomy
neuritis
neurosis
neurotic
neutral
neutrality
neutralization
neutralize
neutralized
neutrally
never
nevermore
nevertheless
new
newcomer
newel
newer
newest
newfangled

newly
newness
newspaper
newsreel
next
nibble
niblick
nice
nicely
niceness
nicer
nicest
nicety
niche
nickel
nickeliferous
nickelodeon
nickname
nicotine
niece
niggard
niggardly
night
nightcap
nightfall
nightgown
nightingale
nightly
nightmare
nightshirt
nighttime

nightwear
nihilism
nihilist
nihilistic
nimble
nimbus
nipper
nipple
nirvana
niter
nitrate
nitric
nitride
nitrification
nitrify
nitrogen
nitrogenous
nitroglycerin
nitrous
no
nobility
noble
nobleman
nobler
noblest
nobly
nobody
nocturnal
nocturnally
nocturne
node

nodule	noncommissioned	nonresident
noel	noncommittal	nonresistance
noise	noncommunicant	nonresistant
noiseless	noncompliance	nonsense
noisier	nonconducting	nonsensical
noisiest	nonconductor	nonsubscriber
noisily	nonconformist	nonsuit
noisiness	nonconformity	nontechnical
noisome	nonconsecutive	nonunion
noisy	noncontagious	nook
nomad	noncorrosive	noon
nomadic	nondescript	noonday
nomenclature	none	noontime
nominal	nonentity	noose
nominally	nonessential	nor
nominate	nonexistence	norm
nominated	nonexplosive	normal
nomination	nonfeasance	normality
nominative	nonfeasor	normally
nominee	nonforfeiture	Norman
nonacceptance	nonfulfillment	Norse
nonadmission	noninter-vention	north
nonagenarian	nonmetallic	northeast
nonagon	nonnegotiable	northeaster
nonappearance	nonpareil	northeasterly
nonattendance	nonparticipating	northeastern
nonce	nonpartisan	northeastward
nonchalance	nonpayment	northerly
nonchalant	nonplus	northern
nonchalantly	nonprofessional	northerner
noncombatant	nonresidence	northernmost

northland	notoriety	nudged
northward	notoriously	nudity
northwest	notwithstanding	nugatory
northwesterly	nought	nugget
northwestern	noun	nuisance
Norwegian	nourish	null
nose	nourished	nullification
noseband	nourishingly	nullify
nosebleed	nourishment	nullity
nosegay	novaculite	numb
nostalgia	novel	number
nostril	novelette	numberless
nostrum	novelist	numbness
not	novelize	numeral
notability	novelty	numerate
notable	November	numeration
notarial	novice	numerator
notary	novitiate	numeric
notation	novocain	numerical
notch	now	numerous
note	nowadays	numismatics
notebook	nowhere	numismatist
noted	noxious	nunnery
noteworthy	noxiousness	nuptial
nothing	nozzle	nurse
nothingness	nuclear	nursemaid
notice	nucleate	nursery
noticeable	nucleation	nurseryman
notification	nucleus	nurture
notify	nude	nutmeg
notion	nudge	nutrient

170

nutriment	nutritive	nuzzled
nutrition	nutritively	nyctalopia
nutritious	nutshell	nymph
nutritiously	nuzzle	nystagmus

O

oaf	objectiveness	obscene
oak	objectivity	obscenity
oaken	objector	obscure
oakum	objurgate	obscured
oar	oblate	obscureness
oarlock	oblation	obscurity
oarsman	obligate	obsequious
oasis	obligation	obsequiously
oaten	obligatory	obsequiousness
oath	oblige	obsequy
oatmeal	obliged	observable
obbligato	obligingly	observance
obduracy	oblique	observant
obdurate	obliquely	observation
obedience	obliqueness	observatory
obedient	obliquity	observe
obeisance	obliterate	observed
obelisk	obliteration	observer
obese	oblivion	observingly
obesity	oblivious	obsess
obey	obliviously	obsession
obituary	obliviousness	obsidian
object	oblong	obsolescence
objection	obloquy	obsolescent
objectionable	obnoxious	obsolete
objective	obnoxiously	obsoletely
objectively	oboe	obsoleteness

172

obstacle	occasional	octet
obstetrical	occasionally	October
obstetrician	occident	octopus
obstinacy	occidental	ocular
obstinate	occipital	oculist
obstinately	occiput	odd
obstreperous	occlude	oddity
obstruct	occlusion	oddly
obstructed	occult	oddness
obstruction	occultation	odeum
obstructionist	occultism	odious
obstructive	occupancy	odiously
obstructor	occupant	odiousness
obtain	occupation	odium
obtainable	occupied	odometer
obtrude	occupy	odor
obtruded	occur	odoriferous
obtruder	occurred	odorless
obtrusion	occurrence	odorous
obtrusive	ocean	oenology
obtuse	oceanic	of
obtusely	oceanography	off
obtuseness	ocelot	offal
obverse	ocher	offcast
obviate	ochlocracy	offend
obviated	octagon	offense
obviation	octagonal	offensive
obvious	octameter	offer
obviously	octangular	offered
ocarina	octave	offerings
occasion	octavo	offertory

173

offhand	oily	onager
office	ointment	once
officer	okra	one
official	old	oneness
officially	olden	onerous
officiate	old-fashioned	oneself
officiated	oldish	onion
officiation	oldness	onlooker
officious	oldster	only
officiously	oleaginous	onomatopoeia
officiousness	oleander	onslaught
offset	oleate	onto
offshoot	oleomargarine	ontology
offshore	olfactory	onus
often	oligarchy	onward
oftentimes	olive	onyx
ogee	omega	ooze
ogive	omelet	oozed
ogle	omelets	opacity
ogled	omen	opal
ogre	ominous	opalesce
ohm	omission	opalescence
ohmage	omit	opalescent
ohmmeter	omnibus	opaque
oil	omnipotence	open
oiled	omnipotent	opened
oiler	omnipresent	opener
oilily	omniscience	openings
oiliness	omniscient	openly
oilskin	omnivorous	openness
oilstone	on	openwork

opera	opprobriously	oratorical
operable	opprobriousness	oratorio
operate	opprobrium	oratory
operated	optic	orb
operatic	optical	orbit
operatically	optician	orchard
operation	optics	orchestra
operative	optimism	orchestral
operator	optimist	orchestrate
operetta	optimistic	orchestrated
ophthalmology	optimistically	orchestration
opiate	optimists	orchid
opinion	optimum	orchidaceous
opinionated	option	ordain
opinionative	optional	ordained
opium	optionally	ordeal
opossum	optometrist	orderliness
opponent	optometry	orderly
opportune	opulence	ordinal
opportunity	opulent	ordinance
oppose	opus	ordinarily
opposed	or	ordinary
opposite	oracle	ordination
opposition	oracular	ordnance
oppress	oracularly	organ
oppression	oral	organic
oppressive	orally	organically
oppressively	orange	organism
oppressiveness	orangeade	organist
oppressor	oration	organization
opprobrious	orator	organize

175

orgy	orphanage	ostracize
orient	orphanhood	ostracized
oriental	orrery	ostrich
orientalism	orthodox	otalgia
orientalist	orthoëpy	other
orientate	orthography	otherwise
orientation	orthopedic	otiose
orifice	ortolan	otitis
origin	oscillate	otorrhea
original	oscillated	otter
originality	oscillation	ottoman
originally	oscillator	ought
originate	oscillatory	ounce
originated	osculate	our
origination	osculation	ours
originative	osculatory	ourselves
originator	osier	oust
oriole	osmium	ouster
Orion	osmosis	out
orlop	osprey	outcast
ormolu	osseous	outclass
ornament	ossification	outcome
ornamental	ossify	outcrop
ornamentally	ostensible	outcroppings
ornamentation	ostensibly	outcry
ornate	ostentation	outcurve
ornithological	ostentatious	outdistance
ornithologist	ostentatiously	outdo
ornithology	osteopath	outdoors
orotund	osteopathy	outer
orphan	ostracism	outermost

176

outfield	outside	overconfident
outfit	outsider	overdevelop
outfitter	outsize	overdo
outflank	outskirt	overdose
outgo	outstandingly	overdraft
outgrowth	outstay	overdress
outings	outstrip	overdriven
outlandish	outtalk	overdue
outlandishness	outward	overestimate
outlast	outwardly	overexpose
outlaw	outwear	overexposure
outlay	outwit	overflow
outlet	oval	overgrown
outlets	ovation	overhand
outline	oven	overhang
outlive	over	overhaul
outlook	overalls	overhead
outmarch	overanxious	overheat
outnumber	overawe	overindulge
outrage	overbalance	overindulgence
outraged	overbear	overissue
outrageous	overbid	overlap
outrageously	overboard	overload
outrageousness	overburden	overlook
outrank	overcapitalize	overlord
outreach	overcast	overmaster
outrider	overcautious	overnight
outrigger	overcharge	overpay
outright	overclothes	overpowered
outrun	overcoat	overpoweringly
outset	overcome	overproduction

177

overrate	overstrain	owe
overrated	oversubscribe	owed
overreach	oversupply	owl
override	overt	owlet
overripe	overtake	owlets
overrule	overthrow	owlish
overrun	overtime	own
overseas	overtone	owned
overseer	overture	owner
overshadow	overturn	ownership
overshadowed	overturned	oxalate
overshoe	overvalue	oxalic
oversight	overweight	oxidation
oversize	overwhelm	oxide
overspread	overwhelmed	oxidize
overstate	overwhelmingly	oxygen
overstatement	overwork	oxyhydrogen
overstep	overwrought	oyster
overstock	ovum	ozone

P

pabulum	pageantry	palfrey
pace	pagination	palimpsest
pacemaker	pagoda	palindrome
pacer	paid	palings
pachyderm	pail	palisade
pacific	pain	pall
pacification	painful	palladium
pacifier	painless	pallbearer
pacifism	painstaking	palliate
pacifist	paint	palliated
pacify	painted	palliation
pack	painter	palliative
package	pair	pallid
packer	paired	pallium
packet	pairings	pallor
packings	pajama	palm
packsaddle	palace	palmetto
pact	palanquin	palmist
pad	palatability	palmistry
paddle	palatable	palpability
paddled	palate	palpable
paddock	palatial	palpate
padlock	palatially	palpation
pagan	palatinate	palpitant
paganism	pale	palpitate
page	paleography	palpitatingly
pageant	palette	palpitation

palsied	pantheon	paralyze
palsy	panther	paralyzed
paltry	pantograph	paramount
pampas	pantomime	paranoia
pamper	pantry	paranoiac
pamphlet	papacy	parapet
pamphlets	papal	paraphernalia
panacea	paper	paraphrase
pancake	papered	paraplegia
panchromatic	papeterie	paraplegic
pancreas	papoose	parasite
pancreatic	paprika	parasitic
panda	parable	parasitical
pandemic	parabola	parasiticide
pandemonium	parabolic	parasol
pander	parabolical	parboil
pandered	parachute	parcel
panegyric	parade	parceled
panegyrical	paradigm	parch
panegyrize	paradise	parchment
panel	paradox	pardon
paneled	paradoxical	pardonable
pang	paraffin	pardoned
panic	paragon	pare
pannier	paragraph	pared
pannikin	parallax	paregoric
panorama	parallel	parent
panoramic	paralleled	parentage
pansy	parallelogram	parental
pant	paralysis	parentheses
pantaloon	paralytic	parenthesis

180

parenthetical	parsnip	paschal
parenthetically	parsonage	pass
parenthood	part	passable
parietal	partake	passage
parings	parted	passageway
parish	parterre	passbook
parishioner	partial	passed
parity	partiality	passenger
park	partially	passion
parka	participant	passionate
parkway	participate	passionately
parlance	participated	passionless
parley	participation	passive
parliament	participator	passivity
parliamentarian	participial	passover
parliamentary	participle	passport
parlor	particle	password
parochial	particular	past
parody	particularity	paste
parole	particularize	pasteboard
paroxysm	particularized	pastel
paroxysmal	particularly	pastern
parquet	partisan	pasteurized
parricidal	partisanship	pastime
parricide	partition	pastor
parrot	partitioned	pastoral
parry	partner	pastorate
parse	partnership	pastrami
parsimonious	partridge	pastry
parsimony	party	pasturage
parsley	parvenu	patch

181

patchwork	patriotic	pawnbroker
patchy	patriotically	pawned
patella	patriotism	pawnshop
patellar	patrol	pay
patent	patrolled	payable
patentable	patrolman	payee
patented	patron	payer
patentee	patronage	paymaster
paternal	patroness	payment
paternalism	patronize	pea
paternally	patronized	peace
paternity	patronymic	peaceable
path	patter	peaceably
pathetic	pattered	peaceful
pathless	pattern	peacemaker
pathologist	patterned	peach
pathology	paucity	peacock
pathos	Paulist	peak
pathway	pauper	peaked
patience	pauperism	peal
patient	pauperization	pealed
patina	pauperize	peanut
patio	pause	pear
patness	paused	pearl
patriarch	pave	pearlite
patriarchal	paved	pearly
patriarchate	pavement	peasant
patrician	pavilion	peasantry
patrimonial	paw	peat
patrimony	pawl	peavey
patriot	pawn	pebble

182

pebbled	pediatrics	peltry
pebbly	pedicular	pelvic
pecan	pediculosis	pelvis
peccadillo	pedigree	pemmican
peccancy	pedigreed	pen
peccant	pediment	penal
peccary	pedometer	penalization
peck	peek	penalize
pectase	peel	penalized
pectin	peeled	penalty
pectoral	peelings	penance
peculate	peep	penchant
peculiar	peer	pencil
peculiarity	peerage	penciled
peculiarly	peered	pendant
pecuniary	peeress	pendency
pedagogic	peerless	pending
pedagogical	peevish	pendulous
pedagogue	peg	pendulum
pedagogy	Pegasus	penetrability
pedal	pelagic	penetrable
pedant	pelf	penetrant
pedantic	pelican	penetrate
pedantical	pelisse	penetration
pedantry	pellagra	penetrative
peddle	pellet	penguin
peddler	pellets	penholder
pedestal	pellucid	penicillin
pedestrian	pelota	penicillium
pedestrianism	pelt	peninsula
pediatrician	pelted	peninsular

183

penitence	peony	percussion
penitent	people	percussive
penitential	peplum	peregrination
penitentiary	pepper	peremptorily
penitently	pepperiness	peremptoriness
penknife	peppermint	peremptory
penman	peppery	perennial
penmanship	pepsin	perfect
pennant	peptic	perfectibility
penniless	peradventure	perfectible
penny	perambulate	perfection
penologist	perambulator	perfectly
penology	perborate	perfidious
pension	percale	perfidy
pensionary	perceivable	perforate
pensioner	perceive	perforation
pensive	per cent	perforator
penstock	percentage	perforce
pent	percentile	perform
pentagon	perceptibility	performable
pentameter	perceptible	performance
Pentateuch	perception	performed
pentathlon	perceptive	performer
Pentecost	perceptual	perfume
penthouse	perch	perfumed
penult	perchance	perfumer
penultimate	percipiency	perfumery
penumbra	percipient	perfunctory
penurious	percolate	pergola
penury	percolation	perhaps
peon	percolator	peril

184

perilous	permeation	persecutor
perilously	permissibility	perseverance
perimeter	permissible	persevere
period	permission	persevered
periodate	permissive	persiflage
periodic	permit	persimmon
periodical	permitted	persist
periodicity	permutation	persistence
peripatetic	permutite	persistency
peripheral	pernicious	persistent
periphery	peroration	persists
periphrastic	peroxide	person
periscope	perpendicular	personable
perish	perpetrate	personage
perishable	perpetration	personal
peristyle	perpetrator	personality
peritoneum	perpetual	personalize
peritonitis	perpetually	personally
periwinkle	perpetuate	personalty
perjure	perpetuated	personification
perjured	perpetuation	personify
perjurer	perpetuator	personnel
perjury	perpetuity	perspective
permanence	perplex	perspicacious
permanent	perplexed	perspicacity
permanently	perplexedly	perspicuous
permanganate	perplexingly	perspiration
permeability	perplexity	perspiratory
permeable	perquisite	perspire
permeate	persecute	perspired
permeated	persecution	persuade

185

persuaded	pessimist	petulant
persuader	pessimistic	petunia
persuasion	pessimists	pew
persuasive	pester	pewter
persuasiveness	pesthouse	phaeton
persulphate	pestiferous	phalanges
pert	pestilence	phalanx
pertain	pestilent	phantasm
pertinacious	pestilential	phantom
pertinacity	pestle	pharmaceutic
pertinence	pet	pharmaceutical
pertinency	petal	pharmacist
pertinent	petaliferous	pharmacol-ogy
perturb	petard	pharmacopoeia
perturbable	petite	pharmacy
perturbation	petition	pharyngitis
perusal	petitioner	pharynx
peruse	petrel	phase
perused	petrifaction	pheasant
Peruvian	petrifactive	phenol
pervade	petrify	phenomena
pervasion	petrol	phenomenal
pervasive	petrolatum	phenomenol-ogy
perverse	petroleum	phenomenon
perversion	petrology	phial
perversity	petticoat	philander
perversive	pettily	philanderer
pervert	pettiness	philanthropic
perverted	pettish	philanthropical
pervious	petty	philanthropist
pessimism	petulance	philanthropy

186

philately	phosphorescence	physiology
philatelic	phosphorescent	physique
philatelist	phosphoric	pianist
philharmonic	phosphorus	piano
philippic	photoelectric	piazza
Philippine	photoengraving	pica
Philistine	photogenic	picaresque
philologist	photograph	piccolo
philology	photographer	pick
philosopher	photographic	pickax
philosophic	photography	picker
philosophical	photogravure	pickerel
philosophize	photolith-ograph	picket
philosophy	photomi-crograph	pickle
philter	photoplay	picklock
phlebitis	photostat	pickpocket
phlebotomy	phrase	pickup
phlegm	phrased	picnic
phlegmatic	phraseology	picnicker
phlox	phrenetic	picric
phobia	phrenic	pictograph
phone	phrenologist	pictorial
phonetic	phrenology	pictorially
phonetician	phthisis	picture
phonetics	phylactery	pictured
phonic	physic	picturesque
phonograph	physical	pie
phosphate	physically	piece
phosphide	physician	piecemeal
phosphite	physics	piecework
phosphoresce	physiognomy	pied

pieplant	pillory	pipe
pier	pillow	pipette
pierce	pillowcase	piquancy
pierced	pilot	piquant
piety	pimento	pique
pig	pimple	piracy
pigeon	pin	piragua
pigeonhole	pinafore	pirate
piggery	pincers	pirated
piggish	pinch	piratic
pigheaded	pincushion	piratical
pigment	pine	pirogue
pigmentation	pineapple	pirouette
pigmy	pinfeather	piscatology
pigskin	pinfish	piscatorial
pigsty	ping-pong	pistachio
pigtail	pinguid	pistol
pigwood	pinhole	piston
pike	pinion	pit
piker	pink	pitch
pikestaff	pinnace	pitcher
pilaster	pinnacle	piteous
pilchard	pinochle	piteousness
pile	pinto	pitfall
piled	pinweed	pith
pilfer	pioneer	pithily
pilgrim	pioneered	pithiness
pilgrimage	pious	pithy
pillage	piously	pitiable
pillar	pip	pitiful
pillion	pipage	pitiless

188

pitilessly	plainly	plateau
pitilessness	plainness	plated
pittance	plaint	plateful
pitted	plaintiff	platen
pituitary	plaintive	plater
pity	plan	platform
pityingly	planchette	platina
pivot	plane	platinate
pivotal	planet	platinic
placability	planetaria	platiniferous
placable	planetarium	platinoid
placard	planetary	platinum
placate	planetoid	platitude
placated	plangent	platitudinize
placatory	plank	platitudinous
place	planked	platoon
placebo	plankton	platter
placeman	planned	platypus
placement	plant	plaudit
placer	plantain	plausibility
placid	plantation	plausible
placidity	planted	play
placidly	planter	player
placket	plantings	playful
plagiarism	plasma	playfulness
plagiarist	plaster	playgoer
plagiarize	plastered	playground
plagiary	plasterer	playings
plague	plastic	playmate
plaid	plasticity	plaything
plain	plate	playtime

189

playwright	pleonastic	plumage
plaza	plethora	plumb
plea	plethoric	plumbago
plead	pleura	plumbate
pleader	pleurisy	plumber
pleadingly	plexus	plumbic
pleadings	pliability	plumbous
pleasant	pliable	plume
pleasantly	pliably	plumed
pleasantness	pliancy	plummet
pleasantry	pliant	plump
please	plier	plumper
pleasurable	pliers	plumpest
pleasure	plight	plumply
plebeian	plinth	plumpness
plebiscite	plodder	plunder
plectrum	plot	plundered
pledge	plotted	plunderer
pledgee	plotter	plunge
pledger	plough	plunged
pledget	plover	plunger
pledgor	plow	plunk
plenary	plowboy	plural
plenarily	plowman	plurality
plenipotentiary	plowshare	pluralize
plenitude	pluck	plus
plenteous	pluckily	plush
plentiful	plucky	plutocracy
plenty	plug	plutocrat
plenum	plugged	plutocratic
pleonasm	plum	plutonic

190

pluvial	poise	politician
ply	poised	politicly
pneumatic	poison	politics
pneumatically	poisoned	polity
pneumatics	poisoner	polka
pneumonia	poisonous	poll
poach	poke	pollen
poacher	poker	pollinate
pocket	pokeweed	pollination
pocketbook	polar	polliniferous
pocketknife	polarity	pollute
pockmark	polarization	polluted
pod	polarize	pollution
podagra	polarized	polo
podiatry	polarizer	polonaise
poem	pole	polonium
poet	polecat	poltroon
poetaster	polemic	polyandrous
poetic	polemical	polyandry
poetical	polemicist	polychrome
poetry	police	polyclinic
poignancy	policeman	polygamist
poignant	policy	polygamous
poinciana	polish	polygamy
poinsettia	polisher	polyglot
point	polite	polygon
pointed	politely	polygonal
pointedly	politeness	polymeric
pointer	politic	polyp
pointless	political	polyphony
pointlessly	politically	polysyllabic

191

polytechnic	poorness	portal
pomade	popcorn	portcullis
pommel	poplar	portend
pomology	poplin	portent
pomp	poppet	portentous
pompadour	poppy	porter
pompano	populace	porterhouse
pomposity	popular	portfolio
pompous	popularity	porthole
poncho	popularization	portico
pond	popularize	portiere
ponder	popularized	portion
ponderable	popularly	portrait
pondered	populate	portraiture
ponderous	populated	portray
pondweed	population	portrayal
pongee	populous	Portuguese
poniard	porcelain	portulaca
pontiff	porch	pose
pontifically	porcupine	poses
pontificate	pore	position
pontoon	pork	positive
pony	pornography	posse
poodle	porosity	possess
pool	porous	possession
pooled	porphyry	possessive
poor	porpoise	possessor
poorer	porringer	possessorship
poorest	port	possibility
poorhouse	portable	possible
poorly	portage	possum

192

post	pot	poundings
postage	potable	pour
postal	potash	pout
postdate	potassium	poverty
postdated	potation	powder
poster	potato	powdered
posterior	potboiler	powdery
posterity	potency	power
postern	potent	powerful
postgraduate	potentate	powerfully
posthaste	potential	powerless
posthumous	potentiality	powerlessly
postilion	potentially	powerlessness
postlude	pothole	powwow
postman	pothook	practicability
postmark	potion	practicable
postmaster	potlatch	practicably
postoperative	potluck	practical
postpaid	potpie	practicality
postpone	potpourri	practically
postponed	potsherd	practice
postponement	pottage	practitioner
postprandial	potter	pragmatic
postscript	pottery	pragmatism
postulant	pouch	pragmatist
postulate	poultice	prairie
postulation	poultry	praise
posture	pounce	praised
postured	pound	praiseworthy
posturings	poundage	praline
posy	poundcake	prance

prank	precipitancy	predict
prate	precipitant	predictable
pratique	precipitate	prediction
prattle	precipitately	predictive
prawn	precipitation	predigest
pray	precipitous	predigestion
prayer	precise	predilection
prayerful	precision	predispose
prayerfully	preclude	predisposed
preach	preclusion	predisposition
preacher	precocious	predominant
preachment	precociously	predominate
preamble	precocity	pre-eminence
prearrange	preconceived	pre-eminent
prearrangement	preconception	pre-empt
prebendary	precursor	pre-emption
precanceled	precursory	preen
precarious	predaceous	preface
precaution	predacity	prefaced
precautionary	predatory	prefatory
precede	predecease	prefect
preceded	predecessor	prefer
precedence	predestination	preferable
precedent	predestine	preferably
precept	predeterminate	preference
preceptor	predetermine	preferential
preceptress	prediastolic	preferentially
precinct	predicament	preferment
precious	predicate	preferred
preciously	predicated	prefix
precipice	predication	preform

pregnancy	prepared	presently
pregnant	preparedness	presentment
prehensile	prepay	preservation
prehistoric	prepayment	preservative
prejudge	preponderance	preserve
prejudice	preponderant	preserver
prejudiced	preponderate	preside
prejudicial	preponderatingly	presidency
prejudicially	preposition	president
prelate	prepositional	presidential
preliminary	prepossess	press
prelude	prepossession	pressboard
premature	preposterous	pressman
premeditate	prerequisite	pressure
premeditated	prerogative	presswork
premeditation	presage	prestidigitator
premier	presbyter	prestige
premise	presbyterian	presto
premises	presbytery	presumable
premium	prescience	presumably
premonition	prescient	presume
premonitory	prescribe	presumed
prenatal	prescribed	presumedly
preoccupation	prescription	presumption
preoccupied	prescriptive	presumptive
preoccupy	presence	presumptuous
prepaid	present	presuppose
preparation	presentability	presystolic
preparative	presentable	pretend
preparatory	presentation	pretended
prepare	presentiment	pretender

195

pretense	prey	primogeniture
pretension	price	primordial
pretensions	priced	primrose
pretentious	prices	prince
preterit	priceless	princeliness
preternatural	prick	princely
pretext	prickle	princes
pretexts	prickliness	princess
prettier	prickly	principal
prettiest	pride	principality
prettily	prideful	principally
prettiness	priest	principle
pretty	priestess	print
pretzel	priesthood	printable
prevail	priestly	printed
prevailed	priggish	printer
prevalence	prim	printery
prevalent	primacy	printings
prevalently	primal	prior
prevaricate	primarily	priority
prevarication	primary	priory
prevaricator	primate	prism
prevent	primateship	prismatic
preventability	prime	prison
preventable	primed	prisoner
prevented	primer	pristine
prevention	primer	privacy
preventive	primeval	private
preview	primitive	privateer
previous	primly	privately
prevision	primness	privateness

196

privation	proclamation	profess
privet	proclivity	professed
privilege	proconsul	professedly
privily	procrastinate	profession
privity	procrastination	professional
privy	procrastinator	professionalism
prize	proctor	professionally
prized	procurable	professor
probability	procuration	professorial
probable	procurator	professorship
probably	procure	proffer
probate	procured	proficiency
probation	procurement	proficient
probationary	prodigal	proficiently
probe	prodigality	profile
probity	prodigious	profit
problem	prodigiously	profitable
problematic	prodigy	profitably
proboscis	produce	profiteer
procedural	produced	profitless
procedure	producer	profligacy
proceed	produces	profligate
proceeded	product	profound
proceedings	production	profoundness
process	productive	profundity
processed	productivity	profuse
processes	proem	profusely
procession	profanation	profuseness
processional	profanatory	profusion
proclaim	profane	progenitor
proclaimed	profanity	progeny

197

prognosis
prognostic
prognosticate
prognostication
program
progress
progression
progressive
prohibit
prohibition
prohibitionist
prohibitory
project
projectile
projection
projector
proletarian
proletariat
proliferate
proliferation
prolific
prolix
prolixity
prologue
prolong
prolongate
prolongation
prolonged
promenade
prominence
prominent

promiscuity
promiscuous
promiscuously
promiscuousness
promise
promisingly
promissory
promontory
promote
promoted
promoter
promotion
prompt
prompted
prompter
promptitude
promptly
promptness
promulgate
promulgation
pronate
pronation
prone
prong
pronghorn
pronominal
pronoun
pronounce
pronounceable
pronounced
pronouncement

pronunciation
proof
prop
propaganda
propagandist
propagate
propagated
propagation
propane
propel
propellant
propelled
propeller
propensity
proper
properly
properties
property
prophecy
prophesied
prophesy
prophet
prophetic
prophetically
prophylactic
prophylaxis
propinquity
propitiate
propitiated
propitiation
propitiatory

198

propitious	prosecutor	protectorate
proponent	proselyte	protein
proportion	proselytize	protest
proportionable	prosily	protestant
proportional	prosiness	protestation
proportionally	prosody	protestingly
proportionate	prospect	protests
proportionately	prospective	prothonotary
proposal	prospector	protocol
propose	prospectus	protoplasm
proposed	prosper	prototype
proposition	prosperity	protoxide
propound	prosperous	protozoa
proprietary	prosperously	protract
proprietor	prosthesis	protraction
propriety	prosthetic	protractive
proptosis	prostrate	protractor
propulsion	prostration	protrude
prorate	prosy	protruded
prorogation	protagonist	protrusion
prorogue	protagonists	protrusive
prorogued	protean	protuberance
prosaic	protect	protuberant
proscenium	protected	proud
proscribe	protectingly	prouder
proscribed	protection	proudest
proscription	protectionist	proudly
prose	protective	provable
prosecute	protectively	prove
prosecuted	protectiveness	provender
prosecution	protector	proverb

199

proverbial	prudence	ptomaine
provide	prudent	public
provided	prudential	publication
providence	prudentially	publicist
provident	prudently	publicity
providential	prudery	publicly
providentially	prudish	publish
provider	prune	publisher
province	pruned	puce
provincial	prurience	puck
provincialism	prurient	pucker
provinciality	Prussian	pudding
provincially	pry	puddle
provision	pryingly	puddled
provisional	psalm	puddler
proviso	psalmist	pudency
provisory	Psalter	pudginess
provocation	pseudonym	pudgy
provocative	psoriasis	pueblo
provoke	psychiatric	puerile
provokingly	psychiatrist	puerility
provost	psychiatry	puff
prow	psychic	puffin
prowess	psychical	puffiness
prowl	psychoanalysis	puffy
proximal	psychological	pug
proximate	psychologist	pugilism
proximity	psychology	pugilist
proximo	psychopathic	pugilistic
proxy	psychopathology	pugnacious
prude	psychosis	pugnaciously

200

pugnacity

puissance

puissant

pull

pulled

pullet

pulley

Pullman

pullulate

pulmonary

pulmotor

pulp

pulpiness

pulpit

pulpiteer

pulpy

pulsate

pulsated

pulsation

pulsator

pulsatory

pulse

pulverization

pulverize

pulverizer

pumice

pump

pumpernickel

pumpkin

pun

punch

puncheon

punctilio

punctilious

punctiliously

punctiliousness

punctual

punctuality

punctually

punctuate

punctuated

punctuation

puncture

punctured

pung

pungency

pungent

puniness

punish

punishable

punishment

punitive

punk

puny

pup

pupa

pupae

pupil

puppet

puppetry

puppy

purblind

purchasable

purchase

purchased

purchaser

pure

purely

purer

purest

purgative

purgatory

purge

purification

purifier

purify

purism

purist

puritan

puritanic

puritanical

Puritanism

purity

purl

purlieu

purloin

purple

purplish

purport

purported

purpose

purposeful

purposeless

purposely	push	puzzle
purr	pushcart	puzzled
purse	pusher	puzzler
purser	pusillanimous	pyelitis
purslane	pustulant	pyemia
pursuance	pustular	pygmy
pursuant	pustulate	pylon
pursue	pustulation	pylorus
pursued	pustule	pyonephrosis
pursuit	put	pyorrhea
pursuivant	putative	pyramid
pursy	putrefaction	pyramidal
purulence	putrefactive	pyre
purulency	putrefy	pyrexia
purulent	putrescence	pyrites
purvey	putrescent	pyrography
purveyance	putrid	pyrometer
purveyor	putt	pyrotechnics
purview	putter	pyroxylin
pus	putty	python

2

quack
quackery
quadrangle
quadratic
quadratics
quadrature
quadrennial
quadrennially
quadrilateral
quadrille
quadruped
quadruple
quadruplex
quadruplicate
quaff
quagmire
quahog
quail
quailed
quaint
quaintly
quaintness
Quaker
qualification
qualified
qualify
qualitative

qualities
quality
qualm
quandary
quantitative
quantities
quantity
quantum
quarantine
quarrel
quarreled
quarrelsome
quarry
quart
quartan
quarter
quartered
quarterly
quartermaster
quartet
quartile
quarto
quartz
quash
quasi
quaternary
quatrain

quaver
quavered
quay
quayage
queen
queenly
queer
quell
quelled
quench
quenchless
querulous
query
quest
question
questionable
questioner
questionnaire
queue
quibble
quick
quicken
quickened
quicklime
quickly
quickness
quicksand

quicksilver	quintessence	quixotic
quiescence	quintet	quiz
quiescent	quip	quizzical
quiet	quipu	quoin
quietly	quire	quoit
quietness	quirk	quondam
quietude	quirt	quorum
quietus	quit	quota
quill	quitclaim	quotable
quilt	quite	quotation
quilted	quitrent	quote
quince	quittance	quoted
quinine	quitter	quoth
quinquennial	quiver	quotidian
quintal	quivered	quotient

R

rabbet

rabbinical

rabbit

rabbitry

rabble

rabid

rabidly

rabies

raccoon

race

raced

racer

raceway

rachitic

rachitis

racial

racially

racily

raciness

rack

racket

raconteur

radial

radially

radiance

radiancy

radiant

radiantly

radiate

radiated

radiation

radiator

radical

radicalism

radically

radii

radio

radiogram

radiophone

radish

radium

radius

radiuses

radon

raffia

raffle

raffled

raft

rafter

raftsman

rag

ragamuffin

rage

ragged

raglan

ragout

ragpicker

ragtime

ragweed

raid

rail

railed

railhead

railings

raillery

railroad

railway

raiment

rain

rainbow

raincoat

rainfall

rainstorm

rainy

raise

raisin

rajah

rake

rakish

rally

ram

ramble	rantingly	rat
rambled	rapacious	ratchet
rambler	rapaciously	rate
ramekin	rapacity	rated
ramification	rapid	rather
ramify	rapidity	rathskeller
rammed	rapidly	ratification
ramp	rapier	ratify
rampage	rapine	ratings
rampant	rapport	ratio
rampart	rapt	ratiocination
ramrod	raptorial	ratiocinative
ramshackle	rapture	ration
ranch	rapturous	rational
rancher	rapturously	rationalism
ranchman	rapturousness	rationalistic
rancho	rarefaction	rationalization
rancid	rarefy	rationalize
rancidity	rarely	rationalized
rancidly	rareness	rationally
rancor	rarity	rationed
rancorous	rascal	ratline
random	rascality	rattan
range	rascally	ratter
ranger	rash	rattle
rank	rasher	rattled
ranked	rashest	rattler
rankle	rashly	rattlesnake
ransack	rashness	rattly
ransom	rasp	raucous
rant	raspberry	ravage

206

ravaged	readings	reappointment
rave	readjust	rear
ravel	readjustment	reared
raveled	readmission	reargue
raven	readmit	rearm
ravenous	ready	rearmament
ravine	reaffirm	rearmed
ravish	reaffirmation	rearmost
ravished	reagent	rearrange
ravishment	real	rearrangement
raw	realism	rearward
rawboned	realist	reason
rawhide	realistic	reasonable
rawness	realistically	reasonableness
ray	reality	reasonably
rayless	realizable	reassemble
rayon	realization	reassert
raze	realize	reasserted
razed	realized	reassign
razor	really	reassigned
razorback	realm	reassume
reach	realtor	reassumed
react	realty	reassurance
reaction	ream	reassure
reactionary	reamer	reassured
read	reanimate	rebate
readability	reap	rebated
readable	reaper	rebel
reader	reappear	rebellion
readily	reappearance	rebellious
readiness	reappoint	rebind

207

rebirth	receiver	reck
reborn	receivership	reckless
rebound	recent	reckon
rebuff	recently	reckoned
rebuild	receptacle	reckoner
rebuilt	receptive	reclaim
rebuke	receptively	reclaimable
rebukingly	receptiveness	reclaimed
rebus	receptivity	reclamation
rebut	recess	recline
rebuttal	recesses	reclined
rebutter	recession	recluse
recalcitrant	recessional	recognition
recall	recessive	recognizable
recalled	recharge	recognizance
recant	recidivism	recognize
recanted	recipe	recognized
recapitalization	recipient	recoil
recapitalize	reciprocal	recoiled
recapitulate	reciprocally	recollect
recapitulated	reciprocate	recollected
recapitulation	reciprocation	recollection
recapture	reciprocative	recommence
recast	reciprocator	recommend
recede	reciprocity	recommendation
receded	recital	recommendatory
receipt	recitalist	recommended
receipted	recitation	recommit
receivable	recitative	recompense
receive	recite	reconcilable
received	recited	reconcile

208

reconciled	recriminative	redden
reconcilement	recriminatory	redder
reconciliation	recrudescence	reddest
reconciliatory	recrudescent	reddish
recondite	recruit	redeem
reconnaissance	recruitment	redeemed
reconnoiter	recrystallize	redeemer
reconnoitered	rectal	redemption
reconquer	rectangle	redemptory
reconquered	rectangular	redirect
reconsider	rectification	redirected
reconstitute	rectifier	rediscount
reconstruct	rectify	rediscover
reconstruction	rectilinear	redistribute
reconstructive	rectitude	redistribution
record	rector	redness
recorded	rectory	redolence
recorder	recumbency	redolent
recordings	recumbent	redouble
recount	recuperate	redoubt
recounted	recuperated	redoubtable
recoup	recuperation	redound
recoupment	recuperative	redress
recourse	recuperatory	reduce
recover	recur	reduced
recoverable	recurred	reducer
recovery	recurrence	reducible
recreant	recurrent	reduction
recreation	recusant	redundance
recriminate	red	redundancy
recrimination	redbreast	redundant

re-echo	refined	refreshingly
reed	refinement	refreshment
reediness	refiner	refrigerant
reedy	refinery	refrigerate
reef	refit	refrigerated
reefer	reflect	refrigeration
reel	reflected	refrigerative
re-elect	reflection	refrigerator
re-embark	reflective	refuge
re-embarkation	reflector	refugee
re-enact	reflex	refulgence
re-enforce	reflexes	refulgent
re-enforcement	reflexive	refund
re-engage	reforestation	refunded
re-engrave	reform	refurnish
re-enlist	reformation	refusal
re-enter	reformative	refuse
re-entry	reformatory	refused
re-establish	reformed	refuses
re-examination	reformer	refutation
re-examine	refract	refute
re-export	refracted	refuted
re-exportation	refraction	regain
refectory	refractive	regained
refer	refractivity	regal
referable	refractor	regale
referee	refractory	regaled
reference	refrain	regalement
referendum	refrained	regalia
referred	refresh	regally
refine	refresher	regard

210

regardful	regretfulness	reinsure
regardless	regrettable	reintroduce
regards	regretted	reinvest
regatta	regular	reinvigorate
regency	regularity	reinvigoration
regeneracy	regularly	reissue
regenerate	regulate	reiterate
regeneration	regulated	reiteration
regenerative	regulates	reiterative
regenerator	regulation	reject
regent	regulator	rejected
regicide	regurgitate	rejection
regimen	regurgitation	rejoice
regiment	rehabilitate	rejoiced
regimental	rehabilitation	rejoices
regimentals	rehearsal	rejoin
regimentation	rehearse	rejoinder
region	reign	rejuvenate
regional	reimburse	rejuvenation
regionally	reimbursed	rejuvenescent
register	reimbursement	rekindle
registered	reimport	relapse
registrar	reimportation	relapsed
registration	rein	relate
registry	reincarnate	related
regress	reincarnation	relation
regression	reindeer	relational
regressive	reinsert	relationship
regret	reinstall	relative
regretful	reinstate	relatively
regretfully	reinsurance	relativity

relator	relish	remittal
relax	relive	remittance
relaxation	reload	remitted
relaxed	relucent	remittent
relaxes	reluctance	remitter
relay	reluctant	remnant
release	reluctantly	remodel
released	rely	remonetize
relegate	remain	remonstrance
relegated	remainder	remonstrant
relegation	remained	remonstrate
relent	remake	remonstrated
relented	remand	remonstration
relentless	remark	remonstrative
relevance	remarkable	remorse
relevancy	remarry	remorseful
relevant	remediable	remorsefully
reliability	remedial	remorseless
reliable	remedied	remote
reliance	remedy	remoteness
reliant	remember	remount
relic	remembered	removability
relief	remembrance	removable
relievable	remind	removal
relieve	reminder	remove
religion	remindful	remunerate
religious	reminiscence	remuneration
religiously	reminiscent	remunerative
relinquish	remiss	renaissance
relinquishment	remission	renal
reliquary	remit	render

212

rendered	reparable	replace
rendezvous	reparation	replaced
rendition	reparative	replacement
renegade	repartee	replant
renew	repast	replenish
renewable	repatriate	replenishment
renewal	repay	replete
renewed	repayment	repletion
rennet	repeal	replevin
renominate	repealed	replica
renominated	repeat	replied
renounce	repeatedly	reply
renovate	repeater	report
renovated	repel	reported
renovation	repelled	reporter
renown	repellence	repose
renowned	repellent	reposed
rent	repent	reposeful
rental	repentance	repository
rented	repentant	repossess
renumber	repented	repossessed
renunciation	repercussion	reprehend
renunciatory	repercussive	reprehensible
reopen	repertoire	reprehension
reorder	repertory	reprehensive
reorganization	repetition	represent
reorganize	repetitious	representation
reorient	repetitive	representative
repaid	rephrase	repress
repair	repine	repression
repaired	repined	repressive

213

reprieve	repugnant	resemblance
reprimand	repulse	resemble
reprimandingly	repulsed	resent
reprint	repulsion	resented
reprinted	repulsive	resentful
reprisal	repurchase	resentfully
reproach	reputable	resentfulness
reproachful	reputation	resentment
reproachfully	repute	reservation
reproachfulness	reputed	reserve
reprobate	reputedly	reserved
reprobation	request	reservist
reproduce	requests	reservoir
reproducer	requiem	resettle
reproduction	require	resettlement
reproductive	requirement	reship
reproof	requires	reshipment
reprove	requisite	reside
reproved	requisition	residence
reprovingly	requital	residency
reptile	requite	resident
reptilian	reredos	residential
republic	rerun	residual
republican	resale	residuary
republicanism	rescind	residue
republicanize	rescinded	residuum
republish	rescript	resign
repudiate	rescue	resignation
repudiated	rescued	resigned
repudiation	research	resignedly
repugnance	resection	resiliency

resilient

resin

resist

resistance

resistant

resistible

resistivity

resistless

resists

resoluble

resolute

resoluteness

resolution

resolvable

resolve

resolved

resolvent

resonance

resonant

resonate

resonator

resort

resorted

resound

resounded

resoundingly

resource

resourceful

resourcefulness

respect

respectability

respectable

respected

respecter

respective

respects

respirable

respiration

respirator

respiratory

respire

respite

resplendence

resplendency

resplendent

respond

responded

respondent

response

responsibility

responsible

responsive

rest

restate

restatement

restaurant

restaurateur

rested

restful

restfully

restfulness

restitution

restive

restively

restiveness

restless

restock

restoration

restorative

restore

restored

restrain

restrained

restrainingly

restraint

restrict

restricted

restriction

restrictive

rests

result

resultant

resumable

resume

resumed

resumption

resurface

resurgence

resurgent

resurrect

resurrected

resurrection

resuscitate

215

resuscitated	retinitis	retroactivity
resuscitation	retinue	retrocession
resuscitative	retire	retrograde
retail	retired	retrogression
retailed	retirement	retrogressive
retailer	retold	retrospect
retain	retort	retrospection
retained	retorted	retrospective
retainer	retouch	retroversion
retake	retoucher	return
retaliate	retrace	returnable
retaliated	retraceable	reunion
retaliation	retract	reunite
retaliative	retracted	revalue
retaliatory	retractile	revamp
retard	retraction	reveal
retardation	retractive	revealed
retarded	retractor	revealingly
retch	retread	revealment
retell	retreat	reveille
retention	retreated	revel
retentive	retrench	revelation
retentivity	retrenchment	reveler
reticence	retrial	revelry
reticent	retribution	revenge
reticle	retributive	revenged
reticular	retrievable	revengeful
reticulate	retrieve	revenue
reticule	retrieved	reverberant
retina	retriever	reverberate
retinal	retroactive	reverberation

216

reverberative	revision	rhapsodize
reverberator	revisit	rhapsody
reverberatory	revitalization	rhenium
revere	revitalize	rheostat
revered	revival	rhesus
reverence	revive	rhetoric
reverend	revived	rhetorical
reverent	revivification	rhetorician
reverential	revivify	rheum
reverie	revocable	rheumatic
reversal	revocation	rheumatism
reverse	revoke	rheumatoid
reversibility	revolt	rhinal
reversible	revolted	rhinestone
reversion	revoltingly	rhinitis
reversionary	revolution	rhinocerous
revert	revolutionary	rhinology
reverted	revolutionist	rhodium
revertible	revolutionize	rhomboid
revetment	revolve	rhombus
revictual	revolved	rhubarb
review	revolver	rhyme
reviewed	revulsion	rhythm
reviewer	revulsive	rhythmic
revile	reward	rhythmical
reviled	rewarded	Rialto
revilement	rewardingly	rib
revilingly	rewrite	ribald
revise	rewritten	ribaldry
revised	rhapsodic	ribbon
reviser	rhapsodist	rice

217

rich	rightly	rip
richer	rightness	riparian
riches	rigid	ripe
richest	rigidity	ripely
richly	rigidly	ripen
richness	rigidness	ripened
rickets	rigor	riper
ricochet	rigorous	ripest
riddance	rile	ripple
ridden	riled	ripply
riddle	rill	riprap
ride	rim	rise
rider	rime	risen
riderless	rind	riser
ridge	ring	risibility
ridicule	ringbolt	risk
ridiculed	ringbone	risky
ridiculous	ringed	rite
ridiculously	ringer	ritual
riffraff	ringingly	ritualistic
riffle	ringleader	ritually
riffled	ringlet	rival
rifled	ringlets	rivalry
rifleman	ringmaster	river
rigger	ringside	riverside
right	rink	rivet
righteous	rinse	rivulet
righteously	riot	roach
righteousness	riotous	road
rightful	riotously	roadbed
rightfully	riotousness	roadhouse

218

roadstead	roguery	roomy
roadster	roguish	roost
roadway	roguishly	rooster
roam	roil	root
roamed	roister	rooted
roamer	roisterer	rooter
roamings	roll	rootlet
roar	rolled	rootlets
roared	roller	rope
roarings	romaine	roquet
roast	Roman	rosaceous
roaster	romance	rosary
rob	Romanesque	rose
robber	romantic	roseate
robbery	romantically	rosette
robin	romanticism	rosewood
robust	romp	rosily
robustly	rompers	rosin
robustness	rondeau	rosiness
rock	roof	roster
rocker	roofer	rostrum
rocket	roofless	rosy
rockweed	rooftree	rot
rocky	rook	Rotarian
rococo	rookery	rotary
rod	room	rotate
rodent	roomed	rotated
rodeo	roomer	rotation
rodman	roomful	rotative
roe	roominess	rotator
rogue	roommate	rotatory

rote	roundsman	rubbish
rotenone	roundworm	rubicund
rotogravure	rouse	ruble
rotor	roused	rubric
rotten	rousingly	ruby
rottenness	rout	rucksack
rotund	route	rudder
rotunda	routed	ruddily
rotundity	routed	ruddiness
rouge	routine	ruddy
rough	rover	rude
roughage	rovings	rudely
roughcast	row	rudeness
roughdry	row	ruder
roughen	rowboat	rudest
roughened	rowdy	rudiment
rougher	rowed	rudimental
roughest	rowel	rudimentary
roughhew	rowen	rueful
roughly	rower	ruff
roughneck	rowlock	ruffian
roughness	royal	ruffle
roughrider	royalism	ruffled
roulade	royalist	Rugby
roulette	royally	rugged
round	royalty	ruin
rounder	rub	ruination
roundest	rubber	ruined
roundhouse	rubberize	ruinous
roundly	rubbery	rule
roundness	rubbings	ruled

220

ruler	rung	rust
rulings	runic	rustic
rum	runner	rusticate
rumble	runt	rustication
ruminant	runway	rusticity
ruminate	rupee	rustily
rumination	rupture	rustiness
ruminative	ruptured	rustle
rummage	rural	rustled
rumor	ruralize	rustler
rumored	rurally	rustlingly
rump	ruse	rusty
rumple	rush	rut
rumpus	rushingly	rutabaga
run	rusk	ruthenium
runabout	russet	ruthless
runc	Russian	rye

$\mathcal{S}$

Sabbatarian

Sabbath

sabbatical

saber

sable

sabotage

saccharin

sachem

sachet

sack

sackcloth

sackful

sacral

sacrament

sacramental

sacred

sacredly

sacredness

sacrifice

sacrificed

sacrificial

sacrilege

sacrilegious

sacristan

sacristy

sacrosanct

sacrum

sad

sadden

sadder

saddest

saddle

saddlebag

saddler

saddlery

sadiron

sadly

sadness

safe

safeguard

safekeeping

safely

safeness

safer

safest

safety

saffron

sag

saga

sagacious

sagaciously

sagacity

sagamore

sage

sagittal

sago

sahib

said

sail

sailboat

sailfish

sailings

sailor

saint

sainted

sainthood

saintliness

saintly

sake

salaam

salability

salable

salacious

salaciously

salaciousness

salad

salamander

salary

sale

saleratus

salesman

salience	salvo	sandman
salient	Samaritan	sandpaper
saliferous	samarium	sandpiper
saline	same	sandstone
saliva	sameness	sandwich
salivate	samite	sandy
salivation	Samoan	sane
sallow	samovar	sanely
sally	sampan	sanguinary
salmon	sample	sanguine
saloon	sampled	sanitarium
salsify	sampler	sanitary
salt	samplings	sanitation
saltcellar	samurai	sanity
salted	sanatorium	Sanskrit
saltpeter	sanatory	sap
salty	sanctification	sapience
salubrious	sanctify	sapient
salubrity	sanctimonious	sapling
salutary	sanctimoniously	saponification
salutation	sanctimoniousness	saponify
salutatorian	sanction	sapper
salutatory	sanctitude	sapphire
salute	sanctity	sapwood
saluted	sanctuary	saraband
salvage	sanctum	Saracen
salvaged	sand	sarcasm
salvation	sandal	sarcastic
salve	sandbag	sarcastically
salve	sandblast	sarcoma
salver	sandiness	sarcophagi

223

sarcophagus	satisfactory	savings
sardine	satisfied	savior
Sardinian	satisfy	savor
sardonic	satisfyingly	savorless
sardonically	satrap	savory
sardonyx	saturate	saw
sarong	saturated	sawdust
sarsaparilla	saturation	sawed
sartorial	Saturday	sawfly
sash	Saturn	sawhorse
sassafras	saturnine	sawmill
sat	satyr	sawn
Satan	sauce	Saxon
satanic	saucepan	say
satchel	saucer	sayings
sateen	saucily	says
satellite	saucy	scab
satiate	saunter	scabbard
satiation	sauntered	scabby
satiety	saunterer	scabies
satin	saurian	scabrous
satinette	sausage	scaffold
satire	sauterne	scald
satiric	savable	scalded
satirical	savage	scale
satirically	savagely	scaled
satirist	savagery	scalene
satirize	savanna	scallion
satirized	savant	scallop
satisfaction	save	scalp
satisfactorily	saved	scalpel

224

scaly	scarification	schizoid
scamp	scarify	schizophrenia
scamper	scarlatina	scholar
scan	scarlet	scholarly
scandal	scathing	scholarship
scandalization	scathingly	scholastic
scandalize	scatter	scholasticism
scandalized	scattered	scholium
scandalous	scatteringly	school
scandalously	scavenger	schoolbook
Scandinavian	scenario	schoolboy
scandium	scene	schoolhouse
scansion	scenery	schoolmaster
scansorial	scenic	schoolmate
scant	scenical	schoolroom
scantily	scent	schoolwork
scantiness	scented	schoolyard
scantling	scepter	schooner
scanty	sceptered	schottische
scapegoat	schedule	sciatica
scaphoid	scheduled	science
scapula	schematic	scientific
scapular	schematize	scientifically
scar	scheme	scientist
scarab	schemed	scimitar
scarce	schemer	scintillant
scarcely	scherzo	scintillate
scarcity	schism	scintillated
scare	schismatic	scintillation
scared	schismatical	scion
scarf	schist	scissors

225

scleritis	scoundrelly	screen
sclerosis	scour	screened
sclerotic	scoured	screenings
sclerotitis	scourge	screw
sclerotomy	scourged	screwed
scoff	scourings	scribble
scoffed	scout	scribbler
scoffer	scouted	scribe
scoffingly	scow	scrimmage
scold	scowl	scrimp
scolded	scowled	scrip
scoldings	scowlingly	script
scone	scramble	scriptural
scoop	scrap	scripture
scoot	scrapbook	scrivener
scooter	scraper	scrod
scope	scrapings	scrofula
scopolamine	scrapple	scrofulous
scorch	scrappy	scroll
scorcher	scratch	scrollwork
scorchingly	scratchiness	scrub
score	scratchy	scrubbed
scored	scrawl	scrubbings
scorn	scrawled	scrubby
scorned	scrawniness	scrummage
scornful	scrawny	scruple
scornfully	scream	scrupulosity
scorpion	screamed	scrupulous
Scot	screech	scrupulously
Scotch	screechy	scrupulousness
scoundrel	screed	scrutinize

226

scrutinized	seal	seaward
scrutinizingly	sealed	sebaceous
scrutiny	sealer	secant
scud	sealskin	secede
scudded	seam	secession
scuff	seaman	secessionist
scuffle	seamanship	seclude
scull	seamless	secluded
sculled	seamstress	seclusion
scullery	seamy	second
scullion	seaplane	secondarily
sculpin	seaport	secondary
sculptor	sear	seconded
sculptural	search	seconder
sculpture	scarcher	secondhand
sculpturesque	searchingly	secondly
scum	searchlight	secrecy
scupper	seared	secret
scurrility	seascape	secretarial
scurrilous	seashore	secretariat
scurrilously	seasick	secretary
scurry	seasickness	secrete
scurvy	seaside	secreted
scuttle	season	secretion
scuttled	seasonable	secretive
scythe	seasonal	secretively
sea	seasonally	secretly
seaboard	seasoned	secretory
seacoast	seasonings	sect
seafarer	seat	sectarian
seafowl	seated	sectarianism

sectary	seducer	segregate
section	seducible	segregated
sectional	seduction	segregation
sectionalism	seductive	seguidilla
sectionalize	seductively	seine
sectionalized	seductiveness	seismic
sectionally	sedulous	seismograph
sector	sedulously	seismology
secular	sedum	seizable
secularism	see	seize
secularize	seed	seizure
secularized	seediness	seldom
secure	seedling	select
secured	seedy	selected
securely	seek	selection
security	seeker	selective
sedan	seem	selectivity
sedate	seemed	selectmen
sedately	seemingly	selector
sedateness	seemliness	selenate
sedative	seemly	selenide
sedentary	seep	selenite
sedge	seepage	selenium
sediment	seersucker	self
sedimentary	seesaw	self-assertion
sedimentation	seethe	self-assured
sedition	seethed	self-colored
seditious	segment	self-command
seditiously	segmental	self-complacency
seditiousness	segmentary	self-complacent
seduce	segmentation	self-conceit

228

self-confidence	self-made	semantic
self-conscious	self-opinionated	semaphore
self-consciousness	self-perception	semblance
self-contained	self-possessed	semester
self-contradiction	self-possession	semiannual
self-contradictory	self-registering	semicircle
self-control	self-reliance	semicircular
self-deceit	self-reliant	semicivilized
self-defense	self-renunciation	semicolon
self-denial	self-reproach	semidetached
self-destruction	self-reproachful	semifinal
self-determination	self-respect	semimonthly
self-determined	self-restraint	seminar
self-educated	self-righteous	seminary
self-esteem	self-righteousness	Seminole
self-evident	self-sacrifice	semiofficial
self-examination	selfsame	semiopaque
self-executing	self-satisfied	semiprecious
self-explaining	self-seeker	Semite
self-explanatory	self-service	Semitic
self-government	self-starter	Semitism
self-help	self-styled	semitone
self-importance	self-sufficiency	semitranslucent
self-induced	self-sufficient	semitransparent
self-indulgence	self-surrender	semiweekly
self-indulgent	self-sustaining	semolina
self-interest	self-winding	sempiternal
selfish	sell	senate
selfishly	sellout	senator
selfishness	Seltzer	senatorial
self-love	selvage	senatorially

senatorship	sensual	separatist
send	sensualism	separatists
sender	sensuality	separative
Seneca	sensually	separator
senescence	sensuous	sepia
senescent	sensuously	sepoy
senile	sensuousness	sepsis
senility	sentence	September
senior	sentenced	septennial
seniority	sententious	septet
senna	sententiously	septic
sennit	sententiousness	septicemia
sensate	sentience	septum
sensation	sentiency	sepulcher
sensational	sentient	sepulchral
sensationalism	sentiently	sepulture
sensationally	sentiment	sequel
sense	sentimental	sequela
senseless	sentimentalism	sequelae
senselessly	sentimentalist	sequence
senselessness	sentimentalists	sequential
sensibility	sentimentality	sequentially
sensible	sentimentally	sequester
sensitive	sentinel	sequestered
sensitively	sentry	sequestrate
sensitiveness	separability	sequestrated
sensitivity	separable	sequestration
sensitization	separate	sequin
sensitize	separated	sequoia
sensitizer	separately	seraglio
sensory	separation	seraph

230

seraphic	servant	severe
seraphical	serve	severely
seraphim	served	severity
Serbian	server	sew
serenade	service	sewage
serenaded	serviceability	sewed
serenata	serviceable	sewer
serene	serviceably	sewerage
serenely	servile	sewn
sereneness	servility	sextant
serenity	servings	sextet
serf	servitor	sexton
serfdom	servitude	shabbiness
serge	sesame	shabby
sergeant	session	shack
scrial	set	shackle
serially	setback	shackled
sericulture	setoff	shade
series	settee	shaded
serif	setter	shadier
serious	settings	shadiest
seriously	settle	shadily
seriousness	settled	shadiness
sermon	settlement	shadings
scrmonize	settler	shadow
sermonized	sever	shadowy
serous	severable	shady
serpent	several	shaft
serpentine	severally	shag
serpiginous	severalty	shaggy
serum	severance	shake

shaken	shape	sheared
shaker	shapeless	shearings
Shakespearean	shapelessly	shears
shakily	shapelessness	sheathe
shakiness	shapeliness	sheathed
shako	shapely	sheave
shaky	shard	shed
shale	share	sheen
shall	shared	sheep
shallop	sharer	sheepish
shallot	shareholder	sheepishly
shallow	shark	sheepishness
shallowly	sharp	sheepskin
shallowness	sharpen	sheer
sham	sharpened	sheerer
shamble	sharpener	sheerest
shame	sharper	sheet
shamed	sharpest	sheetings
shamefaced	sharply	shelf
shameful	sharpness	shell
shamefully	sharpshooter	shellac
shamefulness	shatter	shellfish
shameless	shattered	shellproof
shamelessly	shave	shelter
shamelessness	shaver	sheltered
shampoo	shavings	shelterless
shamrock	shawl	shelve
shanghai	Shawnee	shelved
shank	she	shepherd
shan't	sheaf	Sheraton
shanty	shear	sherbet

232

sheriff	shipwreck	shortage
sherry	shipwright	shortcake
shibboleth	shipyard	shortchange
shield	shire	shortcomings
shift	shirk	shorten
shiftily	shirker	shorter
shiftiness	shirr	shortest
shiftless	shirred	shorthand
shifty	shirt	shortly
shim	shirtings	shortness
shimmer	shiver	shortsighted
shimmered	shivered	shortstop
shimmery	shoal	shot
shin	shock	should
shine	shockingly	shoulder
shiner	shoddy	shouldered
shingle	shoe	shout
shingled	shoes	shouted
Shinto	shook	shove
shiny	shoot	shovel
ship	shootings	shoveled
shipboard	shop	shovelhead
shipbuilder	shopkeeper	show
shipload	shoplifter	showboat
shipmaster	shopman	showed
shipmate	shopper	shower
shipment	shopworn	showered
shipowner	shore	showily
shipper	shored	showiness
shipshape	shorn	showings
shipworm	short	showman

233

shown	shudder	sickeningly
showroom	shuddered	sicker
showy	shudderingly	sickest
shrank	shuffle	sickle
shrapnel	shuffled	sickliness
shred	shun	sickly
shrew	shunned	sickness
shrewd	shunt	side
shrewdly	shut	sideboard
shrewdness	shutdown	sidelong
shriek	shutoff	sidepiece
shrift	shutout	sides
shrike	shutter	sidereal
shrill	shuttered	siderite
shrillness	shuttle	sidesaddle
shrilly	shuttled	sidetrack
shrimp	shy	sidewalk
shrine	shyly	sidings
shrink	shyness	sidle
shrinkage	shyster	sidled
shrinkingly	sialagogue	siege
shrive	Siamese	Sienna
shrivel	sibilance	sierra
shriveled	sibilant	siesta
shroud	sibyl	sieve
shrub	sibylline	sift
shrubbery	Sicilian	sifted
shrug	sick	sigh
shrunk	sickbed	sight
shrunken	sicken	sighted
shuck	sickened	sightless

234

sightliness	silicon	simpered
sightly	silicosis	simple
sigmoid	silk	simpler
signal	silken	simplest
signaled	silkiness	simpleton
signalize	silkweed	simplicity
signalized	silkworm	simplification
signally	silky	simplify
signatory	sill	simply
signature	sillabub	simulacrum
signboard	silliness	simulate
signed	silly	simulation
signer	silo	simultaneous
signet	silt	simultaneously
significance	silvan	sin
significant	silver	since
significantly	silversmith	sincere
signification	silverware	sincerely
signify	silvery	sincerity
signpost	simian	sine
silage	similar	sinecure
silence	similarity	sinew
silenced	similarly	sinewy
silencer	simile	sinful
silent	similitude	sing
silently	simmer	singable
silentness	simmered	singe
silex	simony	singer
silhouette	simoom	single
silica	simoon	singled
silicate	simper	singleness

235

singly	site	skillfully
singular	sitter	skim
singularity	sittings	skimmed
singularly	situated	skimmer
sinister	situation	skimpy
sinistral	sixth	skinflint
sink	sizable	skinny
sinker	size	skip
sinless	sized	skipper
sinlessly	sizes	skirmish
sinned	sizzle	skirmisher
sinner	skate	skirt
sinuosity	skater	skitter
sinuous	skein	skittish
sinus	skeletal	skittishly
sinusitis	skeleton	skittishness
Sioux	skeletonize	skittles
sip	skeptic	skiver
siphon	skeptical	skulk
siphoned	skepticism	skull
sir	sketch	skunk
sire	sketchily	sky
siren	sketchy	skylark
sirloin	skew	skylight
sirocco	skewer	skyrocket
sirup	ski	skyscraper
sister	skid	skyward
sisterhood	skiff	slab
sister-in-law	skill	slack
sisterly	skilled	slacken
sit	skillful	slackened

236

slackness	slayings	slid
slag	sleaziness	slide
slain	sleazy	slier
slake	sled	sliest
slam	sledge	slight
slammed	sleek	slighter
slander	sleekly	slightest
slandered	sleekness	slightingly
slanderer	sleep	slightly
slanderous	sleeper	slightness
slang	sleepily	slim
slangy	sleepiness	slime
slant	sleepless	slimily
slanted	sleeplessness	sliminess
slantingly	sleepy	slimmer
slap	sleet	slimmest
slapdash	sleeve	slimness
slash	sleigh	slimy
slat	sleight	sling
slattern	slender	slink
slatternly	slenderer	slinkiest
slaughter	slenderest	slip
slaughtered	slenderness	slipknot
slaughterer	slept	slippage
slaughterhouse	sleuth	slipper
slave	slew	slipperiness
slavery	slice	slippery
slavish	sliced	slipshod
slaw	slicer	slit
slay	slick	slither
slayer	slicker	sliver

slob	slugger	smash
slobber	sluggish	smashup
sloe	sluggishly	smatter
slog	sluggishness	smear
slogan	sluice	smeared
sloop	sluiceway	smell
slop	slum	smelled
sloppy	slumber	smelt
slosh	slumbered	smelter
slot	slumberer	smilax
sloth	slumberous	smile
slothful	slump	smiled
slothfully	slung	smilingly
slothfulness	slur	smirch
slouch	slurred	smirk
slouchily	slush	smite
slouchiness	slushy	smith
slouchy	sly	smithy
slough	slyly	smitten
slough	smack	smock
slovenliness	small	smoke
slovenly	smaller	smokeless
slow	smallest	smoker
slower	smallness	smokestack
slowest	smallpox	smokiest
slowly	smart	smoky
slowness	smarten	smolder
sloyd	smarter	smoldered
sludge	smartest	smooth
slug	smartly	smoothed
sluggard	smartness	smoother

238

smoothest	snarled	snort
smoothly	snatch	snout
smoothness	snath	snow
smote	sneak	snowball
smother	sneaker	snowbound
smothered	sneakiest	snowdrift
smudge	sneaky	snowdrop
smug	sneer	snowfall
smuggle	sneered	snowflake
smuggled	sneeringly	snowiness
smuggler	sneeze	snowplow
smugly	sneezed	snowshed
smugness	sneezeweed	snowshoe
smut	snicker	snowslide
smuttiest	snickered	snowslip
smutty	sniff	snowstorm
snack	sniffle	snowy
snaffle	sniffled	snub
snag	snip	snuff
snail	snipe	snuffer
snake	snob	snuffle
snaky	snobbery	snug
snap	snobbish	snuggery
snapdragon	snobbishly	snuggle
snapper	snobbishness	snuggled
snappish	snood	snugly
snappy	snoop	snugness
snapshot	snoot	so
snare	snooze	soak
snared	snore	soap
snarl	snored	soapiness

239

soapstone	sodden	solicitation
soapy	sodium	solicitor
soar	sofa	solicitous
soared	soft	solicitude
sob	soften	solid
sober	softer	solidarity
soberly	softest	solidification
sobriety	softly	solidify
sobriquet	softness	solidity
soccer	soggy	solidly
sociability	soil	solidness
sociable	soiled	soliloquize
sociably	sojourn	soliloquy
social	sojourned	solitaire
socialism	solace	solitary
socialist	solar	solitude
socialistic	solarium	solo
socialization	solder	soloist
socialize	soldier	solstice
socialized	soldierly	solubility
socially	soldiery	soluble
socialness	sole	solution
society	solecism	solvable
sociological	solely	solve
sociology	solemn	solvency
sock	solemnity	solvent
socket	solemnization	somber
Socratic	solemnize	sombrero
sod	solemnly	some
soda	solenoid	somebody
sodality	solicit	somehow

240

someone	sophistication	soundless
somersault	sophistry	soundly
something	sophomore	soundness
sometime	soporific	soup
somewhat	soprano	sour
somewhere	sorcerer	source
somnambulism	sorcery	soured
somnambulist	sordid	souse
somnolent	sordidness	south
son	sore	southeast
sonata	sorely	southeasterly
song	sorghum	southeastern
songster	sorority	southerly
sonic	sorosis	southern
son-in-law	sorrow	southerner
sonnet	sorrowful	southernmost
sonority	sorrowfully	southward
sonorous	sorry	southwest
soon	sort	southwesterly
sooner	sorted	souvenir
soonest	sorter	sovereign
soot	sortie	sovereignty
soothe	soubrette	Soviet
soothed	sought	sow
soothingly	soul	sow
soothsayer	soulful	soy
sooty	soulless	soya
sop	soullessly	spa
sophism	soullessness	space
sophist	sound	spacious
sophisticate	sounded	spaciously

241

spaciousness	spatter	speckled
spade	spattered	spectacle
spadefish	spatula	spectacular
spaghetti	spatulate	spectacularly
span	spawn	spectator
spandrel	spawned	specter
spangle	speak	spectral
spangled	speaker	spectroscope
spaniel	spear	spectrum
Spanish	speared	speculate
spank	spearfish	speculated
spanked	spearhead	speculates
spankings	special	speculation
spanner	specialist	speculative
spare	specialization	speculator
spared	specialize	speculatory
sparerib	specialized	speculum
sparingly	specially	speech
spark	specialty	speechless
sparkle	specie	speechlessly
sparkled	species	speechlessness
sparklingly	specific	speed
sparrow	specifically	speedboat
sparse	specification	speedily
sparsely	specify	speedometer
sparsity	specimen	speedway
Spartan	specious	speedy
spasm	speciously	spell
spasmodic	speciousness	spellbound
spasmodically	speck	spelled
spastic	speckle	speller

242

spellings	spinner	splice
spelt	spinneret	splicer
spend	spinster	splint
spendthrift	spinsterhood	splinter
spent	spiny	split
spermaceti	spiral	splurge
spew	spiraled	splutter
sphagnum	spirally	spoil
sphere	spire	spoilage
spherical	spired	spoiled
spheroid	spirit	spoke
sphinx	spirited	spoken
spice	spiritual	spokeshave
spiced	spiritualism	spokesman
spiciness	spiritualist	spoliation
spicy	spirituality	spoliative
spider	spiritualize	spoliator
spidery	spiritually	spondee
spigot	spirituous	sponge
spike	spirochete	sponger
spill	spit	spongy
spilled	spite	sponsor
spillway	spiteful	sponsorship
spin	spittoon	spontaneity
spinach	splash	spontaneous
spinal	spleen	spook
spindle	splendid	spool
spine	splendidly	spoon
spineless	splendor	spoonful
spinet	splendorous	spoor
spinnaker	splenetic	sporadic

243

spore	springy	squad
sport	sprinkle	squadron
sportive	sprinkled	squalid
sportsman	sprinkler	squalidity
sportsmanship	sprint	squalidly
sporty	sprinter	squall
spot	sprite	squalor
spotless	spritsail	squander
spotlessly	sprocket	square
spotlessness	sprout	squared
spotlight	spruce	squarehead
spotted	sprung	squarely
spotter	spry	squareness
spotty	spud	squash
spouse	spume	squat
spout	spun	squatter
sprain	spunk	squaw
sprained	spunky	squawfish
sprawl	spur	squeak
sprawled	spurred	squeal
spray	spurious	squealed
sprayer	spuriously	squeamish
spread	spurn	squeegee
spreader	spurned	squeeze
spree	spurt	squeezed
sprig	spurted	squelch
sprightliness	sputter	squib
sprightly	sputtered	squid
spring	sputum	squint
springboard	spy	squire
springtime	squab	squirm

244

squirmed	stairway	stannous
squirmings	stake	stanza
squirrel	stalactite	staple
squirt	stalagmite	stapler
stab	stale	star
stability	stalemate	starboard
stabilization	stalk	starch
stabilize	stall	starchy
stabilized	stalled	stare
stabilizer	stallion	stared
stable	stamen	starfish
staccato	stamina	stark
stack	stammer	starless
stadia	stammered	starlight
stadium	stammerer	starling
staff	stamp	starred
stag	stampede	starry
stage	stampeded	start
stagecoach	stampings	started
stagecraft	stanch	starter
stagger	stanchion	startle
staggered	stand	startled
stagnant	standard	starvation
stagnate	standardization	starve
stagnation	standardize	state
staid	standpipe	stated
stain	standpoint	statehood
stained	standstill	statehouse
stainless	stank	stateliness
stair	stannate	stately
staircase	stannic	statement

245

stateroom	steak	stenciled
statesman	steal	stenographer
static	stealth	stenographic
station	stealthily	stenography
stationary	steam	stenosis
stationer	steamboat	stentorian
stationery	steamed	step
statistical	steamer	stepchild
statistically	steampipe	stepdaughter
statistician	steamship	stepladder
statistics	steamy	stepmother
statuary	steatite	steppe
statue	steel	stepped
statuesque	steelwork	stepson
statuette	steep	stereopticon
stature	steeper	stereoscope
status	steepest	stereotype
statute	steeple	sterile
statutory	steeplechase	sterility
stave	steeply	sterilization
stay	steepness	sterilize
stayed	steer	sterilized
stead	steerage	sterilizer
steadfast	steered	sterling
steadfastly	steersman	stern
steadfastness	stein	sterner
steadier	stellar	sternest
steadiest	stem	sternly
steadily	stemmed	sternness
steadiness	stench	sternpost
steady	stencil	sternum

246

sternutation	stiletto	stipulate
stertorous	still	stipulated
stet	stillborn	stipulates
stethoscope	stillness	stipulation
stevedore	stilly	stir
stew	stilt	stirred
steward	stilted	stirringly
stick	stimulant	stirrings
sticker	stimulate	stirrup
stickful	stimulated	stitch
stickier	stimulates	stoat
stickiest	stimulation	stock
stickiness	stimuli	stockade
stickler	stimulus	stockbroker
stickpin	sting	stockholder
stickweed	stinger	stockily
sticky	stingier	stockiness
stiff	stingiest	stockinet
stiffen	stingily	stockings
stiffened	stinginess	stockman
stiffness	stingy	stocky
stifle	stink	stockyard
stifled	stinker	stogy
stiflingly	stinkpot	stoic
stigma	stinkweed	stoical
stigmas	stint	stoicism
stigmata	stinted	stoke
stigmatic	stipend	stokehold
stigmatism	stipendiary	stoker
stigmatize	stipple	stole
stile	stippled	stolen

247

stolid

stolidity

stolidly

stomach

stone

stoned

stoneware

stonework

stonily

stoniness

stony

stood

stool

stoop

stop

stopgap

stoppage

stopped

stopper

stopple

storage

store

stored

storehouse

storeroom

stork

storm

stormed

stormy

story

stout

stouter

stoutest

stouthearted

stoutly

stoutness

stove

stow

stowage

stowaway

strabismus

straddle

straddled

straggle

straggled

straggler

straight

straightedge

straighten

straightened

straightforward

straightforwardness

straightway

strain

strained

strainer

strait

straiten

straitened

strake

strand

stranded

strange

strangely

strangeness

stranger

strangest

strangle

strangled

strangler

strangles

strangulate

strangulated

strangulation

strap

strata

stratagem

strategic

strategical

strategist

strategy

stratification

stratify

stratum

stratus

straw

strawberry

stray

streak

streaky

stream

streamed

streamer

streamlet	strikingly	structure
streamlets	string	struggle
streamline	stringed	struggled
street	stringency	struggler
strength	stringent	strum
strengthen	stringently	strummed
strengthened	stringer	strumpet
strenuous	stringpiece	strung
strenuously	stringy	strut
strenuousness	strip	strutted
stress	stripe	strutter
stretch	stripling	strychnine
stretcher	strive	stub
strew	striven	stubble
strewed	strode	stubborn
strewn	stroke	stubby
striate	stroll	stucco
striated	strolled	stuck
striation	stroller	stud
stricken	strong	student
strict	stronger	studied
strictly	strongest	studio
strictness	stronghold	studious
stricture	strongly	study
stride	strontium	stuff
strident	strop	stuffier
stridently	strophe	stuffiest
stridulous	strove	stuffiness
strife	struck	stuffy
strike	structural	stultification
striker	structurally	stultify

249

stumble	stymie	subjectivity
stump	styptic	subjoin
stun	Styx	subjoined
stunned	suasion	subjugate
stunner	suave	subjugation
stunningly	suavely	subjunctive
stunt	suavity	sublease
stunted	subacute	sublet
stupefacient	subaltern	sublimate
stupefaction	subaqueous	sublimated
stupefy	subarctic	sublimation
stupendous	subcaliber	sublime
stupid	subcellar	sublimest
stupidity	subcommittee	subliminal
stupidly	subconscious	sublimity
stupor	subconsciously	subluxation
sturdily	subconsciousness	submarine
sturdiness	subcontract	submerge
sturdy	subcontractor	submersible
sturgeon	subcutaneous	submersion
stutter	subdeacon	submission
stuttered	subdivide	submissive
stutterer	subdivision	submit
sty	subdue	submitted
style	subeditor	subnormal
stylish	subfamily	suboceanic
stylishness	subgroup	subordinate
stylist	subhead	subordination
stylistic	subject	suborn
stylographic	subjection	subornation
stylus	subjective	suborner

250

subpoena	subterraneous	succotash
subscribe	subtitle	succulence
subscribed	subtle	succulent
subscriber	subtler	succumb
subscription	subtlest	such
subsequent	subtlety	suck
subserve	subtly	sucker
subservience	subtract	suckle
subservient	subtracted	suckled
subside	subtraction	suction
subsidence	subtrahend	sudden
subsidiary	subtreasury	suddenly
subsidize	subtropical	suddenness
subsidy	suburb	sudoriferous
subsist	suburban	sudorific
subsistence	suburbanite	sue
subsists	subvention	sued
subsoil	subversion	suède
substance	subversive	suet
substantial	subvert	suffer
substantially	subway	sufferable
substantiate	succeed	sufferance
substantiation	success	suffered
substantive	successful	sufferer
substitute	successfully	sufferings
substituted	succession	suffice
substitution	successive	sufficiency
substratum	successor	sufficient
substructure	succinct	suffix
subterfuge	succinctly	suffocate
subterranean	succor	suffocation

251

suffragan	sulphate	sunbonnet
suffrage	sulphide	sunburn
suffumigate	sulphite	sunburst
suffuse	sulphur	Sunday
suffusion	sulphuric	sunder
sugar	sulphurous	sundial
sugared	sultan	sundry
sugarplum	sultanate	sunfish
sugary	sultry	sunflower
suggest	sum	sunglass
suggestibility	sumac	sunk
suggestible	summarily	sunken
suggestion	summariness	sunless
suggestive	summarization	sunlight
suggestiveness	summarize	sunlit
suicidal	summary	sunned
suicide	summation	sunniness
suicides	summed	sunny
suit	summer	sunrise
suitability	summerhouse	sunset
suitable	summery	sunshade
suite	summit	sunshine
suitor	summon	sunspot
sulk	summoned	sunstroke
sulkily	sump	sup
sulkiness	sumpter	superable
sulky	sumptuary	superabundant
sullen	sumptuous	superannuate
sullenly	sumptuously	superannuation
sullenness	sumptuousness	superb
sully	sunbeam	supercalender

252

supercalendered	supernumerary	supplier
supercargo	superposition	supply
supercharger	supersaturate	support
supercilious	superscription	supporter
superciliously	supersede	suppose
superciliousness	superseded	supposedly
superdreadnought	supersensitive	supposition
supereminent	superstition	suppositious
supererogation	superstitious	suppository
superficial	superstructure	suppress
superficiality	supervene	suppression
superficially	supervened	suppressive
superfluity	supervise	suprarenal
superfluous	supervised	supremacy
superfluously	supervision	supreme
superfluousness	supervisor	supremely
superheat	supervisory	surbase
superhuman	supineness	surcease
superhumanly	supper	surcharge
superimpose	supplant	surcingle
superimposition	supplanted	surd
superinduce	supple	sure
superintend	supplement	surely
superintendence	supplemental	sureness
superintendency	supplementary	surety
superintendent	suppliant	surf
superior	supplicant	surface
superiority	supplicate	surfeit
superlative	supplicated	surge
supernatural	supplication	surgeon
supernaturally	supplicatory	surgery

surgical	survivorship	swarthy
surly	susceptibility	swastika
surmise	susceptible	sway
surmised	suspect	swayed
surmount	suspend	swear
surname	suspended	sweat
surpass	suspender	sweatband
surpassingly	suspense	sweater
surplice	suspension	sweatiness
surplus	suspicion	sweatshop
surprise	suspicious	Swedish
surprised	sustain	sweep
surprisingly	sustained	sweeper
surrebuttal	sustenance	sweepingly
surrebutter	suture	sweepings
surrejoinder	sutured	sweet
surrender	svelte	sweetbread
surreptitious	swab	sweetbrier
surrey	swaddle	sweeten
surrogate	swaddled	sweetened
surround	swag	sweetheart
surrounded	swage	sweetish
surroundings	swagger	sweetly
surtax	swaggered	sweetmeat
surtout	swain	sweetness
surveillance	swallow	swell
survey	swamp	swelled
surveyed	swan	swellings
surveyor	swank	swelter
survival	swanky	sweltered
survive	swarm	swelteringly

254

swerve	sybarite	symposium
swift	sycamore	symptom
swifter	sycophancy	symptomatic
swiftest	sycophant	synagogue
swiftly	sycophantic	synchronize
swiftness	syllabi	synchronous
swill	syllabic	syncopate
swim	syllabicate	syncopation
swimmingly	syllabication	syncope
swindle	syllabification	syndic
swindled	syllabify	syndicalism
swindler	syllable	syndicate
swine	syllabus	syndrome
swineherd	syllabuses	synod
swing	syllogism	synonym
swipe	syllogistic	synonymous
swirl	sylph	synopsis
swirled	sylvan	synoptic
swish	symbol	syntax
Swiss	symbolic	synthesis
switch	symbolical	synthesize
switchboard	symbolism	synthetic
switchman	symbolist	synthetically
swivel	symbolize	syringe
swollen	symmetrical	system
swoon	symmetry	systematic
swoop	sympathetic	systematize
sword	sympathize	systemic
swordfish	sympathizer	systole
swum	sympathy	systolic
swung	symphony	syzygy

255

T

tabasco	tactician	talcum
tabernacle	tactics	tale
tabes	tactile	talebearer
table	tactless	talent
tableau	tactlessly	talented
tablecloth	tadpole	talisman
tablet	taffeta	talk
tablets	taffrail	talkative
tableware	taffy	talker
tabloid	tag	tall
taboo	tagged	taller
tabor	tail	tallest
tabular	tailboard	tallish
tabulate	tailings	tallness
tabulation	tailless	tallow
tabulator	tailor	tally
tachometer	tailpiece	Talmud
tacit	tailrace	talon
tacitly	tailstock	tamarack
taciturn	taint	tamarind
taciturnity	tainted	tambourine
tack	take	tame
tackle	takedown	tamed
tackled	taken	tamer
tact	taker	tamest
tactful	takings	tameness
tactical	talc	tamper

256

tampered	tapestry	tasteful
tampon	tapeworm	tastefully
tan	tapioca	tasteless
tanager	tapir	tastily
tandem	tappet	tasty
tang	tar	tatter
tangent	tarantella	tattered
tangential	tarantula	tattle
tangentiality	tardier	tattled
tangerine	tardiest	tattoo
tangible	tardy	tattooed
tangle	tare	taunt
tangled	target	taunted
tango	tariff	tauntingly
tank	tarlatan	taut
tankage	tarnish	tautological
tankard	tarnished	tautology
tanker	tarpaulin	tavern
tanner	tarpon	tawdry
tannery	tarragon	tawny
tannic	tarred	tax
tantalization	tarry	taxable
tantalize	tart	taxation
tantalized	tartan	taxed
tantalum	task	taxes
Tantalus	taskmaster	taxi
tantamount	Tasmanian	taxicab
tantrum	tassel	taxidermist
tap	tasseled	taxidermy
taper	taste	taximeter
tapered	tasted	taxpayer

257

teach

teachability

teachable

teacher

teacherage

teachings

teacup

teakettle

team

teamster

teamwork

tear

tear

tearful

tearless

tease

teased

teasingly

teaspoon

teaspoonful

technical

technicality

technician

technique

technological

technology

tedious

tediously

tedium

teeter

teetered

teeth

teetotal

teetotaler

telautograph

telecast

telegram

telegraph

telegrapher

telegraphic

telegraphy

telepathic

telepathy

telephone

telephonic

telescope

telescopic

teletype

teleview

televise

television

tell

teller

tellingly

tellings

telltale

tellurium

temerity

temper

temperament

temperamental

temperamentally

temperance

temperate

temperately

temperature

tempest

tempestuous

template

temple

tempo

temporal

temporarily

temporary

temporize

temporized

temporizer

tempt

temptation

tempted

tempter

temptingly

temptress

tenability

tenable

tenacious

tenacity

tenancy

tenant

tenantable

tenanted

tenantless

tenantry

tend	tepidity	terror
tended	tercentenary	terrorism
tendency	teredo	terrorist
tender	tergiversate	terroristic
tendered	term	terrorization
tenderer	termagant	terrorize
tenderest	termed	terse
tenderfoot	terminable	terseness
tenderloin	terminal	tertiary
tenderly	terminate	tessellation
tenderness	terminated	test
tendon	termination	testament
tendril	terminology	testamentary
tenement	terminus	testator
tenet	termite	testify
tennis	termless	testimonial
tenon	tern	testimony
tenor	ternary	tests
tense	terrace	tetanus
tensile	terraced	tether
tension	terrain	tetragon
tent	terrapin	tetragonal
tentacle	terrestrial	tetralogy
tentative	terrible	Teutonic
tenterhooks	terribly	text
tenuity	terrier	textbook
tenuous	terrific	textile
tenuously	terrifically	textual
tenure	terrify	textually
tepee	territorial	texture
tepid	territory	thalamic

thalamus	theodolite	thereunto
thalassic	theologian	thereupon
thallium	theological	therewith
than	theologically	therm
thank	theology	thermal
thankful	theoretic	thermion
thankfully	theoretical	thermite
thankfulness	theoretically	thermometer
thankless	theorist	thermometric
thanklessly	theorize	thermometrical
thanksgiving	theorizer	thermostat
that	theory	thesaurus
thatch	theosophic	these
thaw	theosophical	theses
the	theosophist	thesis
theater	theosophy	thew
theatrical	therapeutic	they
theatrically	therapeutical	thick
theatricals	therapy	thicken
theft	there	thickened
their	thereabout	thickener
theirs	thereafter	thicker
theism	thereat	thickest
them	thereby	thicket
theme	therefore	thickly
themselves	therefrom	thickness
then	therein	thief
thence	thereof	thievery
thenceforth	thereon	thievish
thenceforward	thereto	thigh
theocracy	theretofore	thill

260

thimble	those	thrill
thin	thou	thrillingly
thing	though	throat
things	thought	throatily
think	thoughtful	throatiness
thinkable	thoughtless	throaty
thinker	thoughtlessly	throb
thinly	thoughtlessness	thrombosis
thinner	thousand	thrombus
thinness	thousandfold	throne
thinnest	thrall	throng
third	thrash	throttle
thirst	thrashed	throttled
thirstily	thread	through
thirstiness	threadbare	throughout
thirsty	threadworm	throw
this	threat	thrown
thistle	threaten	thrum
thither	threatened	thrummed
thole	threateningly	thrush
thong	three	thrust
thoracic	threnody	thud
thorax	thresh	thug
thorium	threshold	thulium
thorn	threw	thumb
thorny	thrice	thump
thorough	thrift	thunder
thoroughbred	thriftily	thunderbolt
thoroughfare	thriftless	thundered
thoroughly	thriftlessness	thunderous
thoroughness	thrifty	thundershower

261

Thursday	tighten	tincture
thus	tightened	tinctured
thwack	tightener	tinder
thwart	tighter	tine
thy	tightest	tinge
thyme	tightly	tinged
thymus	tightrope	tingle
thyroid	tightwad	tingled
thyself	tile	tinker
tiara	tiled	tinkle
tibia	till	tinkled
tick	tiller	tinned
ticker	tilt	tinnitus
ticket	tilted	tinny
tickle	timber	tinsel
tickled	time	tinsmith
tickler	timed	tint
ticklish	timekeeper	tinted
tidal	timeless	tintinnabulation
tide	timeliness	tinware
tidewater	timely	tiny
tideway	timepiece	tip
tidily	timer	tippet
tidiness	timetable	tipple
tidings	timid	tippler
tidy	timidity	tipsy
tie	timidly	tiptoe
tier	timorous	tiptop
tiffin	timorously	tirade
tiger	tin	tire
tight	tinct	tired

262

tireless	toast	tomato
tirelessly	toasted	tomb
tiresome	tobacco	tomboy
tiresomely	toboggan	tombstone
tiresomeness	toccata	tomorrow
tissue	tocsin	ton
Titan	today	tonal
titanic	toddle	tonality
titaniferous	toddled	tone
titanium	toddy	toneless
tithe	toe	tongs
titillate	toenail	tongue
titillated	toffee	tonic
titillation	toga	tonight
titivate	together	tonnage
titivated	toggle	tonneau
titivation	toil	tonsil
title	toiled	tonsillitis
titled	toiler	tonsorial
titmouse	toilet	tonsure
titrate	toilets	tontine
titration	token	too
titter	told	took
tittered	tolerable	tool
titular	tolerance	tooth
titulary	tolerant	toothache
to	tolerate	toothbrush
toad	tolerated	toothed
toadfish	toleration	toothless
toadstool	toll	toothpick
toady	tomahawk	toothsome

263

top	torque	touchable
topaz	torrent	touchdown
topcoat	torrential	touchily
topiary	torrentially	touchiness
topic	torrid	touchingly
topical	torridity	touchstone
topknot	torsion	touchy
topmast	torso	tough
topmost	tort	toughen
topographer	tortoise	toughened
topographic	tortuously	tougher
topographical	tortuousness	toughest
topography	torture	tour
topple	tortured	toured
toppled	torturer	tourist
topsail	Tory	tourists
toque	toss	tourmaline
torch	tossup	tournament
torchwood	total	tourniquet
tore	totaled	tousle
toreador	totalitarian	tousled
torment	totality	tow
tormented	totalization	towage
tormentingly	totally	toward
tormentor	totem	towards
tornado	totter	towboat
torpedo	tottered	towel
torpid	totteringly	tower
torpidity	tottery	towered
torpidly	toucan	toweringly
torpor	touch	towline

town	traditionally	transact
township	traffic	transacted
toxic	trafficked	transaction
toxicity	tragedian	transatlantic
toxicology	tragedy	transcend
toxicosis	tragic	transcendence
toy	tragical	transcendency
trace	tragus	transcendent
traceable	trail	transcendental
tracer	trailed	transcribe
tracery	trailer	transcribed
trachea	train	transcript
tracheal	trained	transcription
trachoma	trainer	transept
tracings	trainman	transfer
track	trait	transferable
trackage	traitor	transference
trackless	traitorous	transferred
trackman	traitorously	transfiguration
tract	trajectory	transfigure
tractability	tram	transfigured
tractable	trammel	transfix
traction	trammeled	transform
tractive	tramp	transformation
tractor	trample	transformed
trade	trampled	transformer
traded	tramway	transfusion
trader	trance	transgress
tradesman	tranquil	transgression
tradition	tranquillity	transgressor
traditional	tranquilly	transient

265

transit	transplantation	trawl
transition	transport	trawler
transitional	transportation	tray
transitionally	transported	treacherous
transitive	transposal	treacherously
transitory	transpose	treacherousness
translatable	transposed	treachery
translate	transposition	treacle
translation	transship	tread
translator	transshipment	treadle
transliterate	transubstantiation	treadmill
translucence	transverse	treason
translucent	trap	treasonable
transmigration	trapdoor	treasure
transmissible	trapeze	treasured
transmission	trapezoid	treasurer
transmit	trapper	treasury
transmittal	trappings	treat
transmitter	Trappist	treated
transmogrify	trash	treatise
transmutable	trashy	treatment
transmutation	trauma	treaty
transmute	traumata	treble
transmuted	traumatic	tree
transom	travail	trek
transparency	travel	trellis
transparent	traveled	tremble
transpiration	traveler	tremblingly
transpire	travelogue	tremblings
transpired	traverse	tremendous
transplant	travesty	tremendously

266

tremolo	tributary	trinity
tremor	tribute	trinket
tremulous	triceps	trinomial
tremulously	trichinosis	trio
tremulousness	trick	trip
trench	trickery	tripe
trenchancy	trickily	tripthong
trenchant	trickiness	triple
trenchantly	trickle	triplet
trencher	trickled	triplets
trend	trickster	triplex
trepan	tricky	triplicate
trephine	tricot	triplication
trepidation	tricycle	triply
trespass	trident	tripod
trespasser	tried	trippingly
trestle	triennial	trireme
trestlework	trifle	trisect
triad	trifled	triturate
trial	trifler	trituration
triangle	trigger	triumph
triangular	trigonometry	triumphal
triangulate	trill	triumphant
triangulation	trilled	triumvir
tribal	trillion	triumvirate
tribasic	trillium	triune
tribe	trilogy	trivalent
tribesman	trim	trivial
tribulation	trimmed	triviality
tribunal	trimmer	trivially
tribune	trimness	trochaic

267

troche	truckle	trustworthiness
troll	truckled	trustworthy
trolley	truckman	trusty
trombone	truculence	truth
troop	truculent	truthful
troopship	trudge	truthfully
trophy	trudged	truthfulness
tropic	true	try
tropical	trueness	tryst
tropically	truffle	tub
trot	truism	tuba
troth	truly	tube
trotter	trump	tuber
troubadour	trumped	tubercle
trouble	trumpery	tubercular
troublesome	trumpet	tuberculin
troublingly	trumpeter	tuberculosis
troublous	trumpetweed	tuberculous
trough	truncate	tuberose
trounce	truncated	tubular
troupe	truncheon	Tuesday
trousers	trundle	tuft
trousseau	trunk	tug
trout	trunnion	tuition
trowel	truss	tularemia
truancy	trust	tulip
truant	trustee	tulipwood
truce	trusteeship	tulle
truck	trustful	tumble
truckage	trustfully	tumbler
trucked	trustfulness	tumor

268

tumult	turgidly	tutorial
tumultuous	Turk	twain
tumultuously	turkey	twang
tumulus	turmeric	twanged
tun	turmoil	tweak
tuna	turn	tweed
tundra	turnbuckle	tweezers
tune	turncoat	twice
tuned	turned	twiddle
tuneful	turner	twiddled
tuneless	turnings	twig
tuner	turnip	twilight
tungsten	turnkey	twill
tunic	turnout	twin
tunnel	turnover	twinborn
tunneled	turnpike	twine
tunny	turnstile	twined
turban	turpentine	twinge
turbid	turpitude	twinkle
turbidity	turquoise	twinkled
turbidly	turret	twirl
turbinate	turreted	twirled
turbine	turtle	twist
turbot	Tuscan	twistings
turbulence	tusk	twit
turbulent	tussle	twitch
turbulently	tussled	twitted
tureen	tutelage	twitter
turf	tutelary	twittered
turgid	tutor	twitteringly
turgidity	tutored	two

twofold		typhoon		typography	
twosome		typhous		typothetae	
tycoon		typhus		tyrannical	
type		typical		tyrannicide	
typed		typification		tyrannize	
typesetter		typify		tyrannous	
typewriter		typist		tyranny	
typewritten		typographer		tyrant	
typhoid		typographic		tyro	

270

U

ubiquitous	umlaut	unassisted
udder	umpire	unassuming
ugliness	umpired	unattached
ugly	unable	unattainable
ukase	unabridged	unattempted
ukulele	unaccented	unattended
ulcer	unacceptable	unauthenticated
ulcerate	unaccompanied	unauthorized
ulceration	unaccountable	unavailable
ulcerative	unaccustomed	unavoidable
ulcerous	unadjusted	unaware
ulna	unadorned	unbalanced
ulnar	unadulterated	unballasted
ulster	unaffected	unbar
ulterior	unaided	unbecomingly
ultimate	unalloyed	unbeknown
ultimately	unalterable	unbeknownst
ultimatum	un-American	unbelief
ultimo	unamiable	unbelievable
ultramarine	unanimous	unbeliever
ultramodern	unanswerable	unbend
ultraviolet	unappeasable	unbendingly
ululate	unapproachable	unbiased
ululation	unappropriated	unbidden
umber	unarmed	unbind
umbrage	unasked	unblemished
umbrella	unassailable	unblushing

271

unbolted	unclassified	uncontrollable
unborn	uncle	unconventional
unbosom	unclean	uncork
unbound	uncleaned	uncounted
unbounded	unclosed	uncouple
unbowed	unclothed	uncouth
unbreakable	uncoil	uncover
unbridled	uncoiled	uncovered
unbuckle	uncollectible	unction
unbuckled	uncomfortable	unctuous
unbusinesslike	uncomfortably	uncultivated
unbutton	uncommon	uncut
uncage	uncommunicative	undamaged
uncanny	uncompanionable	undamped
unceasingly	uncomplimentary	undaunted
unceremonious	uncompromising	undeceive
unceremoniously	unconcealed	undeceived
uncertain	unconcerned	undecided
uncertainly	unconditional	undecipherable
uncertainty	unconditionally	undeciphered
unchallenged	unconfined	undefended
unchangeable	uncongenial	undefiled
uncharitable	unconquerable	undemonstrative
unchecked	unconquered	undeniable
unchristened	unconscionable	under
unchristian	unconscious	underbid
uncivil	unconsciously	underbrush
uncivilized	unconsciousness	undercharge
unclad	unconsidered	underclothes
unclaimed	unconstitutional	undercurrent
unclasp	uncontradicted	undercut

272

underdose	understandingly	undiscriminating
underestimate	understate	undisguised
underexpose	understatement	undismayed
undergarment	understood	undisposed
underglaze	understudy	undisputed
undergo	undertake	undistinguishable
undergraduate	undertaken	undisturbed
underground	undertaker	undivided
undergrowth	undertone	undo
underhanded	undertook	undone
underlaid	undertow	undoubted
underlie	undervalue	undress
underline	underwater	undrinkable
underling	underwear	undulant
undermine	underwent	undulate
underneath	underworld	undulation
underpaid	underwrite	undulous
underpass	underwriter	undutiful
underpay	underwritten	undying
underpinning	undeserved	unearned
underproduction	undesigned	unearth
underrate	undesired	unearthly
underscore	undestroyed	uneasiness
undersell	undetermined	uneasy
undershirt	undeveloped	uneatable
undershot	undigested	uneaten
undersigned	undignified	uneducated
undersized	undimmed	unembarrassed
underskirt	undisciplined	unemployment
underslung	undisclosed	unencumbered
understand	undiscovered	unendangered

273

unending
unendorsed
unendurable
unenforceable
unenterprising
unenvied
unequal
unequaled
unequally
unequipped
unequivocal
unerring
unessential
unestimated
unethical
uneven
uneventful
unexampled
unexcelled
unexceptionable
unexpected
unexpectedly
unexpectedness
unfaded
unfair
unfairly
unfairness
unfaithful
unfaithfulness
unfaltering
unfamiliar

unfashionable
unfasten
unfastened
unfavorable
unfeeling
unfeelingly
unfeigned
unfermented
unfettered
unfilled
unfinished
unfit
unflattering
unflinchingly
unfold
unforeseen
unforgettable
unforgivable
unformed
unfortified
unfortunate
unfortunately
unfrequented
unfriendly
unfruitful
unfunded
unfurl
unfurled
unfurnished
ungainly
ungodly

ungovernable
ungracious
ungrammatical
ungrateful
ungratefully
ungratefulness
ungrudgingly
unguarded
unguent
unguided
unhackneyed
unhampered
unhandy
unhanged
unhappiness
unhappy
unhardened
unharness
unhatched
unhealthful
unhealthy
unheard
unheeded
unheedful
unhesitatingly
unhinge
unhitch
unholy
unhonored
unhook
unhoped

unhorse	uninterrupted	unlace
unhurt	uninviting	unladylike
unhygienic	union	unlatch
unicorn	unionism	unlaundered
unidentified	unionist	unlearn
unification	unionization	unlearned
uniform	unionize	unleash
uniformed	unionized	unleavened
uniformity	unique	unless
uniformly	uniquely	unlettered
unify	uniqueness	unlicensed
unilateral	unison	unlike
unilluminated	unissued	unlikely
unimaginable	unit	unlimited
unimaginative	Unitarian	unlisted
unimpaired	unitary	unlock
unimpeachable	unite	unlocked
unimportant	united	unlooked
unimpressionable	unity	unlovable
unimproved	universal	unluckily
unincorporated	universality	unlucky
uninformed	universally	unmake
uninhabitable	universe	unmanageable
uninhabited	university	unmanly
uninitiated	unjustifiable	unmannerly
uninjured	unkind	unmarried
uninstructed	unkindliness	unmask
unintelligent	unknightly	unmatched
unintelligible	unknowable	unmentionable
unintentional	unknowingly	unmerciful
unintentionally	unknown	unmercifully

275

unmindful   unpopular   unrepentant

unmistakable   unpracticed   unreproved

unmixed   unprecedented   unrequited

unmolested   unprejudiced   unreserved

unmounted   unpremeditated   unreservedly

unnamed   unprepared   unresisting

unnatural   unpreparedness   unrestrained

unnecessary   unprepossessing   unrestricted

unnerve   unpretentious   unrewarded

unnumbered   unprincipled   unrighteous

unobjectionable   unprofessional   unripe

unobservant   unprogressive   unrivaled

unobserved   unpromising   unroll

unobtainable   unproved   unruffled

unoccupied   unpublished   unruly

unopened   unpunctual   unsaddle

unopposed   unqualified   unsafe

unorganized   unquestionable   unsaid

unpack   unquestionably   unsalable

unpaid   unquestioned   unsanctified

unpalatable   unreasonable   unsatisfactory

unparalleled   unreasonably   unsatisfied

unpardonable   unrebuked   unsavory

unpardoned   unrecognizable   unscrew

unparliamentary   unrecognized   unscrewed

unpaved   unreconciled   unscrupulous

unperturbed   unredeemed   unseasonable

unpleasant   unrelated   unseasoned

unplowed   unremitting   unseemly

unpolished   unremunerative   unseen

unpolluted   unrepaired   unselfish

unselfishly

unsettle

unsettled

unshakable

unshaven

unsheathe

unsheltered

unship

unshorn

unsightly

unsigned

unskilled

unskillful

unsmirched

unsnarl

unsociable

unsoiled

unsoldierly

unsolicited

unsophisticated

unsought

unsound

unspeakable

unspoken

unsportsmanlike

unstable

unstained

unsteadily

unsteady

unstrung

unsubstantial

unsubstantiated

unsuccessful

unsuitable

unsung

unsure

unsuspected

unsweetened

unswerving

unsympathetic

unsystematic

untangle

untangled

untainted

unteachable

untechnical

untenanted

untested

unthinkable

unthinking

unthinkingly

untidily

untidy

untie

until

untiringly

unto

untold

untouched

untoward

untracked

untranslatable

untried

untroubled

untrue

untruth

untruthful

untutored

untwine

untwist

unusable

unused

unusual

unusually

unutterable

unuttered

unvalued

unvarnished

unvarying

unveil

unversed

unwarrantable

unwarranted

unwary

unwarily

unwashed

unwaveringly

unwearied

unwelcome

unwell

unwholesome

unwieldy

unwilling

unwillingly	uprising	usefulness
unwillingness	uproar	useless
unwind	uproarious	uselessly
unwise	uproot	uselessness
unwittingly	upset	user
unwonted	upshot	uses
unworkable	upside	usher
unworldly	upstairs	usual
unworthy	upstart	usually
unwrap	uptake	usufruct
unwreathe	uptown	usurer
unwritten	upturn	usurious
up	upturned	usurp
upas	upward	usurper
upbraid	uranium	usury
upgrowth	urban	utensil
upheaval	urbane	utilitarian
upheld	urbanely	utilitarianism
uphill	urbanity	utilities
uphold	urchin	utility
upholder	urge	utilizable
upholster	urged	utilization
upholsterer	urgency	utilize
upholstery	urgent	utilized
upkeep	urgently	utmost
uplift	urn	Utopia
upmost	usable	Utopian
upon	usage	utter
upper	use	utterance
uppermost	useful	uttered
upright	usefully	utterly

278

$\mathcal{V}$

vacancy

vacant

vacate

vacation

vacationist

vaccinate

vaccination

vaccine

vacillate

vacillatingly

vacillation

vacuity

vacuous

vacuum

vagabond

vagary

vagrancy

vagrant

vague

vagus

vain

vainglorious

vainglory

vainly

vainness

valance

valedictorian

valedictory

valence

valentine

valerian

valet

valiant

valid

validate

validated

validation

validity

validly

valise

valley

valor

valorous

valuable

valuation

value

valued

valueless

valve

valvular

valvulitis

vampire

vanadium

vandal

vandalism

vane

vanguard

vanilla

vanish

vanity

vanquish

vantage

vapid

vapidly

vapor

vaporization

vaporize

vaporized

vaporizer

vaporous

variability

variable

variance

variant

variation

varicose

varicosity

varied

variegate

variegation

variety

variola	vehicular	venomously
various	veil	ventilate
variously	veiled	ventilation
varnish	vein	ventilator
vary	veined	ventral
vascular	veinlet	ventricle
vase	vellum	ventricular
vaseline	velocipede	venture
vassal	velocity	ventured
vassalage	velure	venturesome
vast	velvet	venue
vat	velveteen	veracious
Vatican	velvety	veracity
vaudeville	venal	veranda
vault	venality	verb
vaulted	vend	verbal
vector	vendee	verbalization
vedette	vender	verbalize
veer	vendible	verbalized
veered	vendor	verbally
vegetable	veneer	verbatim
vegetarian	venerable	verbiage
vegetarianism	venerate	verbose
vegetate	venerated	verbosity
vegetated	veneration	verdant
vegetation	vengeance	verdict
vegetative	vengeful	verdigris
vehemence	venial	verdure
vehement	venially	verge
vehemently	venison	verged
vehicle	venom	verification

280

verify	vertigo	vibrated
verily	verve	vibration
verisimilitude	very	vibrator
veritable	vesicle	vibratory
veritably	vesper	vicar
verity	vessel	vicarage
vermicelli	vest	vicarious
vermicide	vestal	vicariously
vermiform	vested	vice
vermifuge	vestibular	viceregal
vermilion	vestibule	viceroy
vermin	vestige	vicinity
verminous	vestigial	vicious
vernacular	vestment	viciously
vernal	vestry	vicissitude
vernier	veteran	victim
versatile	veterinarian	victimize
versatility	veterinary	victimized
verse	veto	victor
versification	vex	Victorian
versifier	vexation	victorious
versify	vexatious	victoriously
version	vexed	victory
verso	viability	victual
versus	viable	victualed
vertebra	viaduct	video
vertebrae	vial	vie
vertebrate	viand	vied
vertex	vibrancy	view
vertical	vibrant	viewed
vertically	vibrate	vigil

vigilance

vigilant

vigilantly

vignette

vigor

vigorous

vigorously

vile

viler

vilest

vilification

vilify

villa

village

villager

vinaigrette

vinculum

vindicable

vindicate

vindication

vindictive

vine

vinegar

vineyard

vintage

vinylite

viol

violate

violated

violation

violative

violator

violence

violent

violently

violet

violets

violin

violinist

viper

virago

vireo

virgin

virginal

virginity

virile

virility

virtual

virtually

virtue

virtuosity

virtuoso

virtuous

virulence

virulency

virulent

virus

visa

visage

viscera

visceral

viscid

viscidity

viscose

viscosity

viscount

viscous

vise

visibility

visible

vision

visionary

visit

visitation

visited

visitor

vista

visual

visualization

visualize

visualized

visually

vital

vitality

vitalize

vitalized

vitally

vitamin

vitiate

vitiated

vitiation

vitreous

vitrification

282

vitrify	voided	vomited
vitriol	volatile	vomitory
vituperate	volatility	voodoo
vituperation	volatilization	voracious
vituperative	volatilize	voracity
vivacious	volcanic	vortex
vivaciously	volcano	vortical
vivacity	volition	votary
vivid	volitional	vote
vividly	volley	voter
vivisection	volt	votive
vixen	voltage	vouch
vocabulary	voltameter	vouched
vocal	voltammeter	voucher
vocalism	voltmeter	vouchsafe
vocalist	volubility	vow
vocalization	voluble	vowed
vocalize	volubly	vowel
vocalized	volume	voyage
vocally	volumetric	vulcanization
vocation	voluminous	vulcanize
vocationally	voluntarily	vulgar
vocative	voluntary	vulgarian
vociferous	volunteer	vulgarism
vodka	voluptuary	vulgarity
vogue	voluptuous	vulgarize
voice	voluptuously	vulgarized
voiced	volute	vulgarly
voiceless	volvulus	vulnerability
void	vomica	vulnerable
voidable	vomit	vulture

W

wad	waitress	wandered
waddle	waive	wanderer
wade	waiver	wane
waded	wake	waned
wader	wakeful	wangle
wafer	wakefully	want
waffle	wakefulness	wanted
waft	waken	war
wag	wale	warble
wage	walk	warbler
waged	walker	ward
wager	walkout	warded
wagered	walkover	warden
waggle	wall	warder
waggled	walled	wardrobe
wagon	wallet	wardroom
waif	wallets	warehouse
wail	wallflower	warfare
wailed	wallow	warily
wailings	wallpaper	wariness
wainscot	walnut	warlike
waist	walrus	warm
waistband	waltz	warmed
waistline	wampum	warmly
wait	wan	warmth
waited	wand	warn
waiter	wander	warned

284

warningly	watchcase	waveringly
warp	watchdog	waviness
warrant	watchful	wavy
warranted	watchfully	wax
warrantor	watchfulness	waxen
warranty	watchmaker	waxiness
warren	watchman	waxwing
warship	watchtower	waxy
wart	watchword	way
wary	water	waybill
was	watered	wayfarer
wash	waterfall	waylaid
washable	waterfowl	waylay
washcloth	waterlogged	wayside
washer	Waterloo	wayward
washout	watermark	waywardness
washroom	waterproof	we
washstand	watershed	weak
washwoman	waterside	weaken
wasp	waterspout	weakened
waspish	waterway	weaker
wassail	waterworks	weakest
wastage	watery	weakling
waste	watt	weakly
wastebasket	wattage	weakness
wasted	wattle	wealth
wasteful	wattled	wealthier
wastefully	wattmeter	wealthiest
wastefulness	wave	wealthy
wastrel	waver	weapon
watch	wavered	wear

285

wearable	weigh	whack
wearer	weighings	whale
wearily	weight	whaleback
weariness	weighty	whalebone
wearings	weir	whaler
weary	weird	wharf
weasel	weirdly	wharfage
weather	weirdness	wharfinger
weatherboard	welcome	what
weathercock	welcomed	whatever
weathered	weld	whatnot
weatherproof	welded	whatsoever
weave	welfare	wheat
weaver	well	wheaten
web	welt	wheatworm
webbing	welter	wheedle
wed	weltered	wheedled
wedded	wen	wheel
wedding	wench	wheelbarrow
wedge	wend	wheeled
wedged	wended	wheelwright
wedlock	went	wheeze
Wednesday	wept	whelk
weed	were	whelp
weedy	west	when
week	westerly	whence
weekday	western	whenever
weekly	westerner	whensoever
weep	westward	where
weevil	wet	whereabouts
weft	wetness	whereas

286

whereat	whip	whittle
whereby	whipcord	whittled
wherefore	whippet	who
wherefrom	whipstitch	whoever
wherein	whipstock	whole
whereof	whipworm	wholehearted
whereon	whir	wholesale
wheresoever	whirl	wholesaler
whereupon	whirled	wholesome
wherever	whirligig	wholesomely
wherewith	whirlpool	wholly
wherewithal	whirlwind	whoop
wherry	whisk	whose
whet	whisker	whosoever
whetted	whisky	why
whether	whisper	wick
which	whispered	wicked
whichever	whisperer	wickedness
whichsoever	whist	wicker
whiff	whistle	wickerwork
Whig	whistled	wicket
while	white	wide
whilom	whitecap	widen
whim	whitefish	wider
whimper	whiten	widespread
whimpered	whiteness	widest
whimsey	whitewash	widow
whimsical	whitewings	widowed
whimsically	whitewood	widower
whine	whither	widowhood
whined	whitlow	width

287

wield	windlass	wise
wife	windmill	wiseacre
wig	window	wisely
wiggle	windowpane	wiser
wiggled	windpipe	wisest
wigwag	windrow	wish
wigwam	windstorm	wished
wild	windward	wishful
wilderness	windy	wishfully
wildfire	wine	wisp
wildness	wineglass	wistful
wile	wing	wistfully
will	winged	wistfulness
willed	wingless	wit
willful	wink	witch
willfully	winked	witchcraft
willfulness	winkle	witchery
willingly	winner	with
willingness	winningly	withal
willow	winnings	withdraw
wily	winnow	withdrawal
win	winsome	withdrew
wince	winter	wither
winch	wipe	withered
wind	wiper	witheringly
windage	wire	withhold
windbreak	wired	within
windfall	wireless	without
windily	wirepulling	withstand
windings	wireworm	witless
windjammer	wisdom	witness

288

witticism	wonderwork	workman
wittingly	wondrous	workmanship
witty	wondrously	workmen
wives	won't	workshop
wizard	wont	workwoman
wizardly	woo	workwomen
wizardry	wood	world
wizened	woodchuck	worldliness
woe	wooded	worldly
woebegone	wooden	worm
woeful	woodland	wormwood
woefully	woodman	wormy
wolf	woodpecker	worn
wolfhound	woodsman	worried
wolfish	woodwork	worrier
wolverene	woodworm	worriment
wolves	wooer	worrisome
woman	woof	worry
womanhood	wool	worse
womankind	woolen	worship
womanlike	wooliness	worshiped
womanliness	woolly	worshiper
womanly	word	worshipful
women	wordiness	worst
won	wordy	worsted
wonder	work	worsted
wonderful	workable	worth
wonderfully	worked	worthily
wonderingly	worker	worthiness
wonderland	workhouse	worthless
wonderment	workings	worthy

289

would	wrecker	writ
wound	wren	write
wound	wrench	writer
wove	wrest	writhe
woven	wrestle	writings
wrack	wrestled	written
wraith	wrestler	wrong
wrangle	wretch	wrongful
wrangled	wretchedly	wrongfully
wrap	wretchedness	wrongheaded
wrapper	wriggle	wrongly
wrappings	wriggled	wrongness
wrath	wring	wrote
wrathful	wringer	wroth
wrathfully	wrinkle	wrought
wreath	wrinkled	wrung
wreck	wrist	wry
wreckage	wristlet	wryneck

X   Y   Z

xenon	yearling	young
xeroderma	yearly	younger
xerosis	yearn	youngest
X-ray	yearningly	youngish
xylophone	yearnings	youngster
xyster	yeast	your
	yeasty	yourself
yacht	yell	yourselves
yachtsman	yelled	youthful
yak	yellow	youthfully
Yale	yelp	youthfulness
yam	yeoman	ytterbium
yank	yeomanry	yttrium
Yankee	yes	yucca
yard	yesterday	yule
yardage	yet	yuletide
yardarm	yew	
yardstick	yield	zany
yarn	yielded	zeal
yarrow	yieldingly	zealot
yaw	yodel	zealotry
yawl	yoga	zealously
yawn	yolk	zebra
ye	yon	zebu
yea	yonder	zenith
year	yore	zephyr
yearbook	you	Zeppelin

zero	Zionism	zone
zest	Zionist	zoo
zigzag	zipper	zoological
zinc	zirconium	Zulu
Zion	zodiac	zymology

PART TWO

PERSONAL AND GEOGRAPHICAL NAMES

Part Two consists of 2,604 entries of personal and geographical names divided approximately as follows:

1,600 geographical names. The largest group of names consists of the names of American cities and towns that are likely to be encountered in business dictation. The names of the American states and territories are given. A relatively small group of foreign geographical names is given—the foreign countries and cities that are most likely to occur in American business dictation. The lists are not intended to be complete or exhaustive. The attempt has been made, however, to include the geographical names that occur most frequently in ordinary business dictation.

350 surnames. This small group of last names represents the commonest American last names that are likely to be used in business dictation. There are tens of thousands of surnames in this country, and no attempt can be made to present a complete list.

350 first names of women. This list contains the more frequently used feminine first names.

350 first names of men. This list contains the more frequently used masculine first names.

The four groups of names listed above are combined in one alphabetical list in Part Two.

With the exception of the states and of a few of the largest cities, the geographical names are written very fully. This is done with the understanding that the writer will use these full outlines for the names that occur only occasionally in the dictation. When some name occurs more frequently in the dictation, an abbreviated form will be used.

The shorthand writer in Oregon would ordinarily have little occasion to use the outline for *Corpus Christi*. The Texan shorthand writer might use it so frequently that he would abbreviate it to *kk*.

In order to keep the list in Part Two as short and at the same time as useful as possible the names of many cities and towns are omitted. This is possible because many American city and town names are composed of nouns and adjectives that appear in Part One — such names as *White River Junction* or *Egg Harbor City*.

Many cities and towns form their names by adding to the name of another town a word like *Beach, Grove, Hill, City, Park,* or *Spring*. In most cases such names have been omitted as they would cause no shorthand writing difficulty.

PERSONAL AND GEOGRAPHICAL NAMES

Aaron	Alabama	Alliance
Abbott	Alameda	Allison
Abel	Alamosa	Alma
Aberdeen	Alan	Alonso
Abigail	Alaska	Alpena
Abilene	Albania	Alphonsine
Abington	Albany	Alphonso
Abner	Albert	Althea
Abraham	Alberta	Alton
Abram	Albia	Altoona
Ada	Albion	Altus
Adam	Albuquerque	Alva
Adams	Alcoa	Alvin
Adelaide	Alexander	Amanda
Adelbert	Alexandra	Amarillo
Adler	Alexandria	Ambridge
Adolph	Alexis	Ambrose
Adrian	Alfred	Amelia
Adrienne	Algeria	Americus
Afghanistan	Algernon	Ames
Africa	Alhambra	Amesbury
Agatha	Alice	Amherst
Agnes	Alicia	Amityville
Aiken	Aliquippa	Amos
Aileen	Allan	Amsterdam
Ainsworth	Allen	Amy
Akron	Allentown	Anaconda

295

Anacortes	Arcadia	Attleboro
Anaheim	Archer	Aubrey
Anastasia	Archibald	Auckland
Andalusia	Ardmore	Audry
Anderson	Argentina	Audubon
Andover	Arizona	Augusta
Andrews	Arkadelphia	Augustin
Angela	Arkansas	Aurelia
Angelica	Arline	Aurelius
Angora	Arlington	Aurora
Angus	Armstrong	Austin
Anita	Arnold	Australia
Ann	Arthur	Austria
Anna	Asa	Avalon
Annabel	Asbury Park	Avery
Annapolis	Asheboro	Avis
Ann Arbor	Asheville	Ayres
Annette	Ashland	Azusa
Anniston	Ashley	Bacon
Anoka	Ashtabula	Bailey
Anselm	Astoria	Bainbridge
Ansonia	Asunción	Baird
Anthony	Atchison	Baker
Antigo	Athelstan	Bakersfield
Antioch	Athena	Baldwin
Antoinette	Athens	Ballard
Antonia	Athol	Baltimore
Antwerp	Atkinson	Bangkok
Appleton	Atlanta	Bangor
Arabella	Atlantic	Baptist
Arabia	Atlantic City	Baptista

296

Baraboo

Barbara

Barberton

Barcelona

Barlow

Barnabas

Barnaby

Barnard

Barnesville

Barnett

Barnstable

Barranquilla

Bartholomew

Barre

Barrett

Barrington

Bartlesville

Bartlett

Bartow

Basil

Bastrop

Batavia

Batesville

Bath

Baton Rouge

Battle Creek

Bauer

Baxter

Bayard

Bay City

Bayonne

Beacon

Beale

Beardstown

Beatrice

Beaumont

Beaver

Beaver Dam

Beaver Falls

Becker

Beckley

Bedford

Beecher

Belfast

Belgium

Belinda

Bell

Bella

Bellaire

Belle

Bellefontaine

Bellefonte

Belleville

Bellevue

Bellingham

Bellwood

Belmont

Beloit

Belvedere

Bemidji

Bend

Benedict

Benedicta

Bender

Benjamin

Bennett

Bennington

Benson

Bentley

Benton

Benton Harbor

Berea

Bergenfield

Berkeley

Berlin

Bernard

Bernstein

Bertha

Bertram

Bertrand

Berwick

Berwyn

Beryl

Bessemer

Bessie

Bethlehem

Beulah

Beverly

Bicknell

Biddeford

Big Spring

Billings

Biloxi

297

Binghamton	Boonville	Brian
Birmingham	Bordeaux	Bridgeport
Bisbee	Boris	Bridget
Bishop	Boston	Bridgeton
Bismarck	Bosworth	Bridgewater
Bissell	Boulder	Briggs
Blackstone	Bound Brook	Brigham
Blackwell	Bowen	Brisbane
Blair	Bowling Green	Bristol
Blairsville	Bowman	Bristow
Blake	Boyd	Brockton
Blakely	Boyle	Bronxville
Blanchard	Bozeman	Brookfield
Blanche	Brackenridge	Brookhaven
Bliss	Braddock	Brookings
Bloomfield	Bradenton	Brown
Bloomington	Bradford	Brownsville
Bloomsburg	Bradley	Brownwood
Bluefield	Brady	Bruce
Blue Island	Brainerd	Bruno
Bluffton	Braintree	Brunswick
Blytheville	Brattleboro	Brussels
Bogalusa	Brawley	Bryan
Bogota	Brazil	Bryant
Boise	Bremen	Bucharest
Bolivia	Bremerton	Bucyrus
Bombay	Brenham	Budapest
Bonham	Brennan	Buenos Aires
Boniface	Brentwood	Buffalo
Boone	Brewer	Bulgaria
Boonton	Brewster	Burbank

Burke	Camilla	Cartersville
Burley	Campbell	Carthage
Burlingame	Campeche	Casper
Burlington	Canada	Catharine
Burma	Canal Zone	Cathleen
Burns	Canfield	Catskill
Burrillville	Cannon	Cecelia
Burroughs	Canon City	Cecil
Burton	Canonsburg	Cedar Falls
Butler	Canton	Cedarhurst
Butte	Cape Girardeau	Cedar Rapids
Byron	Cape Town	Cedartown
Cable	Caracas	Cedric
Cadillac	Carbondale	Celeste
Cadwallader	Carey	Celestine
Caesar	Carlisle	Celia
Cairo	Carlotta	Centerville
Calais	Carlsbad	Central Falls
Calcutta	Carlson	Centralia
Caldwell	Carlstadt	Ceylon
Caleb	Carlton	Chalmers
Calexico	Carmel	Chambersburg
Calgary	Carmen	Champaign
Calhoun	Carnegie	Chandler
California	Carol	Chanute
Callahan	Carpenter	Chapman
Calumet City	Carroll	Chariton
Calvin	Carrollton	Charleroi
Cambridge	Carson	Charles
Camden	Carter	Charleston
Cameron	Carteret	Charlotte

Charlottesville	Cicely	Clifton Forge
Chase	Cicero	Clinton
Chattanooga	Cincinnati	Cloquet
Chauncy	Circleville	Clotilda
Cheboygan	Clairton	Clovis
Chelsea	Clara	Coaldale
Cheltenham	Clare	Coatesville
Cherbourg	Claremont	Cobb
Cherokee	Clarence	Coddington
Chester	Claribel	Coeur d'Alene
Cheviot	Clarice	Coffeyville
Cheyenne	Clarinda	Cohen
Chicago	Clark	Cohoes
Chickasha	Clarksburg	Colby
Chico	Clarksdale	Coldwater
Chicopee	Clarksville	Coleman
Chihuahua	Claudia	College Park
Childress	Claudius	Collier
Childs	Claudine	Collingdale
Chile	Clayton	Collingswood
Chillicothe	Clearfield	Collins
China	Clearwater	Collinsville
Chippewa Falls	Cleary	Cologne
Chisholm	Cleburne	Colombia
Christabel	Clement	Colorado
Christchurch	Clementina	Colorado Springs
Christian	Clementine	Colton
Christina	Cleveland	Columbia
Christine	Clifford	Columbia Heights
Christopher	Cliffside Park	Columbus
Chula Vista	Clifton	Compton

300

Comstock	Corinna	Cudahy
Concord	Corinth	Culbertson
Concordia	Cork	Cullman
Condon	Cornelia	Culver City
Cone	Cornelius	Cumberland
Conklin	Corning	Cummings
Conley	Corona	Cummins
Connecticut	Coronado	Curtis
Connellsville	Corpus Christi	Cushing
Connelly	Corry	Cuthbert
Connersville	Corsicana	Cutler
Connolly	Cortland	Cynthia
Connor	Corvallis	Cyril
Conrad	Corwin	Cyrus
Conshohocken	Coshocton	Czechoslovakia
Constance	Costa Rica	Dagmar
Constant	Council Bluffs	Dallas
Constantine	Covington	Dalton
Constantinople	Grafton	Daly
Conway	Craig	Dan
Cook	Crandall	Danbury
Cooley	Cranford	Daniel
Coolidge	Cranston	Daphne
Cooper	Crawford	Davenport
Copenhagen	Crawfordsville	Danville
Cora	Creston	Darby
Coral Gables	Crispin	Darlington
Coraopolis	Cromwell	Dartmouth
Corbin	Crookston	David
Cordele	Crowley	Davidson
Cordelia	Cuba	Davis

Dawson	Des Moines	Dover
Dayton	De Soto	Dowagiac
Daytona Beach	Detroit	Downers Grove
Dean	Devils Lake	Doyle
Dearborn	Dewey	Dresden
Deborah	Dexter	Driscoll
Decatur	Diana	Drusilla
Decker	Dick	Dublin
Decorah	Dickinson	Du Bois
Dedham	Dickson City	Dubuque
Deerfield	Dillon	Dudley
Defiance	Dinah	Duffy
De Kalb	District of Columbia	Dulcie
De Land	Dix	Duluth
Delaware	Dixon	Dumont
Delhi	Dobbs Ferry	Dunbar
Delia	Dodge City	Duncan
Della	Dolores	Dunn
Delphine	Dominic	Dunellen
Delphos	Dominican Republic	Dunkirk
Del Rio	Donald	Dunmore
Demetrius	Donora	Duquesne
Denise	Donovan	Durango
Denison	Dora	Durant
Denmark	Dorcas	Durham
Dennison	Doris	Duryea
Denton	Dormont	Dwight
Denver	Dorothea	Dyersburg
De Pere	Dorothy	Eagle Pass
Depew	Dougherty	Earl
Derby	Douglas	Easley

East Aurora	Effingham	Eloise
East Chicago	Egan	El Paso
Easthampton	Egbert	El Reno
East Hartford	Egypt	Elsa
East Lansing	Eileen	El Salvador
Eastman	Eire	Elsie
East Moline	Elaine	Elspeth
Easton	Elbert	Elton
East Orange	Elberton	Elvira
East Peoria	Eldred	Elwood
East Pittsburgh	El Centro	Ely
East Point	El Cerrito	Elyria
East Providence	Eleanor	Emery
East Rochester	Electra	Emil
East Rutherford	Elgin	Emily
East Stroudsburg	Elihu	Emma
Eau Claire	Elijah	Emmanuel
Ebenezer	Elisha	Emporia
Ecuador	Elizabeth	Endicott
Edgar	Elizabethton	England
Edina	Elk City	Englewood
Edinburgh	Elkhart	Enid
Edith	Elkins	Ennis
Edmonton	Ellen	Enos
Edmund	Ellensburg	Enrico
Edna	Elliott	Enright
Edward	Ellsworth	Ephraim
Edwardsville	Ellwood City	Ephrata
Edwin	Elmer	Erasmus
Edwina	Elmhurst	Erastus
Effie	Elmira	Eric

303

Erie	Evelina	Fitchburg
Erma	Evelyn	Fitzgerald
Ernest	Everard	Flagstaff
Ernestine	Everett	Flat River
Erwin	Exeter	Flavia
Escanaba	Ezra	Fleming
Estella	Fairbanks	Flint
Esther	Fairbury	Flora
Estherville	Fairfield	Florence
Esthonia	Fairhaven	Florida
Ethan	Fairlawn	Floyd
Ethel	Fairmont	Flynn
Ethiopia	Fairview	Foley
Etna	Faith	Fond du Lac
Etta	Fall River	Ford
Euclid	Falls City	Ford City
Eudora	Fargo	Forest City
Eugene	Farrell	Forest Park
Eugenia	Fayetteville	Forest Hills
Eulalia	Feldman	Fort Atkinson
Eunice	Felix	Fort Collins
Euphemia	Ferdinand	Fort Dodge
Eureka	Fergus Falls	Fort Lauderdale
Europe	Ferguson	Fort Lee
Eustace	Ferndale	Fort Madison
Eva	Fidelia	Fort Myers
Evangeline	Field	Fort Pierce
Evanston	Findlay	Fort Scott
Evansville	Finland	Fort Smith
Eve	Finley	Fort Thomas
Eveleth	Fisher	Fort Wayne

304

Fort Worth	Gaffney	Gifford
Foster	Gail	Gilbert
Fostoria	Gainesville	Girard
Fox	Galesburg	Gladys
Framingham	Galion	Glasgow
France	Gallagher	Glassport
Frances	Gallup	Gleason
Francis	Galveston	Glencoe
Frankfort	Garden City	Glen Cove
Franklin	Gardiner	Glendale
Fraser	Gardner	Glenn
Frederic	Garfield	Glenna
Frederica	Garret	Glen Ridge
Fredericksburg	Gary	Glen Rock
Fredericton	Gasper	Glens Falls
Freehold	Gastonia	Globe
Freeland	Geneva	Gloria
Freeman	Genevieve	Gloucester
Freeport	Genoa	Gloversville
Fremont	Geoffrey	Goddard
French	George	Godfrey
Fredonia	Georgetown	Goldberg
Fresno	Georgia	Goldsboro
Frieda	Gerald	Goodwin
Frostburg	Geraldine	Gordon
Fuller	Gerard	Goshen
Fullerton	Germany	Gould
Fulton	Gertrude	Grace
Gabriel	Gettysburg	Grafton
Gabriella	Gibson	Graham
Gadsden	Gideon	Grand Forks

Grand Haven   Grosse Pointe   Harding

Grand Island   Grove City   Harlan

Grand Junction   Grover   Harley

Grand Rapids   Guadalajara   Harold

Grant   Guam   Harper

Grants Pass   Guatemala   Harriet

Graves   Gulfport   Harriman

Gray   Gustavus   Harrington

Great Barrington   Gutenberg   Harris

Great Britain   Guthrie   Harrisburg

Great Falls   Guy   Harrison

Great Neck   Hackensack   Harrisonburg

Greece   Haddonfield   Hartford

Greeley   Haddon Heights   Hartman

Green   Hagerstown   Hartsville

Green Bay   Haggerty   Harvey

Greenfield   Haiti   Hasbrouck

Greensboro   Halifax   Hastings Heights

Greensburg   Hall   Hattiesburg

Greenville   Hamburg   Havana

Greenwood   Hamilton   Haverford

Gregory   Hammond   Haverstraw

Grenada   Hampton   Havre

Greta   Hancock   Hawaii

Gretchen   Hanford   Hawthorne

Gretna   Hannah   Hays

Griffin   Hannibal   Hayward

Griffiths   Hanover   Hazard

Grinnell   Hans   Healy

Griselda   Hansen   Hector

Gross   Hanson   Hedwig

Helen	Hoffman	Hudson
Helena	Holdenville	Hugh
Heloise	Holland	Hughes
Hempstead	Hollywood	Hugo
Henderson	Holmes	Huldah
Henrietta	Holt	Humboldt
Henry	Holyoke	Humphrey
Herbert	Homer	Hungary
Herkimer	Homestead	Hunter
Herman	Homewood	Huntington
Hermosa Beach	Honduras	Huntsville
Herrin	Honesdale	Huron
Hester	Hong Kong	Hutchinson
Hezckiah	Honolulu	Hyattsville
Hibbing	Hoover	Iceland
Hickory	Hope	Ichabod
Higgins	Hopewell	Ida
Highland Park	Hopkins	Idaho
High Point	Hopkinsville	Idaho Falls
Hilda	Horace	Ignatius
Hill	Horatio	Illinois
Hillsboro	Hornel	Imogene
Hillsdale	Hortense	Independence
Hillside	Horton	India
Hingham	Hosea	Indiana
Hinsdale	Hot Springs	Indianapolis
Hinton	Houston	Inglewood
Hiram	Howard	Iola
Hobart	Howell	Iowa
Hoboken	Hubbs	Iowa City
Hodges	Hubert	Ipswich

307

Ira	Jamaica	Joan
Iran	James	Job
Iraq	Jamestown	Jocelin
Ireland	Jane	Jock
Irene	Janesville	Joel
Iris	Janet	John
Irma	Janice	Johnson
Iron Mountain	Japan	Johnston
Ironton	Jared	Johnstown
Ironwood	Jarvis	Joliet
Irving	Jason	Jonah
Irvington	Jasper	Jonas
Irwin	Jean	Jonathan
Isaac	Jeannette	Jones
Isabel	Jefferson	Jonesboro
Isadora	Jeffersonville	Joplin
Ishpeming	Jeffrey	Joseph
Isidore	Jemima	Joyce
Isolde	Jenkins	Judah
Israel	Jenkintown	Jude
Istanbul	Jennifer	Judith
Italy	Jennings	Julia
Ithaca	Jenny	Julian
Ivan	Jeremiah	Juliana
Ivy	Jerome	Juliet
Jabez	Jersey City	Julius
Jack	Jerusalem	June
Jackson	Jessamine	Junius
Jacksonville	Jesse	Justin
Jacobs	Jessica	Justina
Jacqueline	Jessie	Kabul

308

Kalamazoo	Keyport	Lake City
Kalispell	Keyser	Lake Forest
Kane	Key West	Lakeland
Kankakee	Kharkov	Lake Wales
Kansas	Kilgore	Lakewood
Kansas City	Kimball	Lake Worth
Karen	King	Lambert
Karl	Kingsford	Lancaster
Kate	Kingston	Lancelot
Katharine	Kingsville	Lanett
Kathleen	Kinston	Lansdale
Kawanee	Kirksville	Lansdowne
Kearny	Kirkwood	Lansford
Keene	Kittanning	Lansing
Keith	Kitty	La Paz
Kelly	Klamath Falls	Lapeer
Kelso	Klein	La Porte
Kelvin	Knight	Laramie
Kendallville	Knox	Larchmont
Kenmore	Knoxville	Laredo
Kennedy	Kokomo	Larksville
Kenneth	Korea	Lars
Kennett	Laban	Larson
Kenosha	Lacey	La Salle
Kent	Lackawanna	Las Cruces
Kenton	Laconia	Las Vegas
Kentucky	La Crosse	Latrobe
Keokuk	La Grande	Latvia
Kerr	Lafayette	Laughlin
Kerrville	La Junta	Laura
Kester	Lake Charles	Laurel

309

Laurens	Leroy	Llewellyn
Laurinburg	Leslie	Lloyd
Lavinia	Lester	Lockhart
Lawrence	Letitia	Lock Haven
Lawrenceville	Lettice	Lockport
Lawton	Levy	Lodi
Lazarus	Lewis	Logan
Lead	Lewiston	Logansport
Leah	Lewistown	Lois
Leander	Lexington	Lola
Leavenworth	Libby	Lombard
Lebanon	Liberia	London
Lederer	Liechtenstein	Long
Lee	Lillian	Long Beach
Leeds	Lilly	Long Branch
Lehighton	Lima	Longview
Lehman	Limon	Lorain
Leipsig	Lincoln	Lorenzo
Lelia	Linden	Loretta
Le Mars	Lindstrom	Lorinda
Lemuel	Linton	Los Angeles
Lena	Lionel	Louis
Leningrad	Lisa	Louisa
Lenoir	Lisbon	Louise
Leo	Litchfield	Louisiana
Leominster	Lithuania	Louisville
Leon	Little Falls	Loveland
Leonard	Little Rock	Lowell
Leonia	Liverpool	Lubbock
Leonora	Livingston	Lucinda
Leopold	Livingstone	Lucius

310

Lucretia	Mahoney	Marilla
Lucy	Maine	Marinette
Ludington	Malden	Marion
Ludlow	Malone	Marlboro
Luella	Malvern	Marlin
Lufkin	Malverne	Marquette
Luke	Manchester	Marseilles
Lumberton	Mandan	Marshall
Luther	Mandy	Marshalltown
Luxembourg	Manhattan	Marshfield
Luzerne	Manila	Martha
Lydia	Manistee	Martin
Lyle	Manistique	Martinez
Lynbrook	Manitoba	Martinsburg
Lynch	Manitowoc	Martinsville
Lynchburg	Mankato	Maryville
Lyndhurst	Mannheim	Mason
Lynn	Manuel	Mason City
Lynwood	Manzala	Massachusetts
Lyons	Maple Heights	Massena
Mabel	Maplewood	Massillon
Mack	Marblehead	Mathilda
Madeline	Marcella	Matthew
Madge	Marcellus	Mattoon
Madison	Marcia	Maud
Madisonville	Marcus	Maurice
Madrid	Margaret	Maximilian
Mae	Marguery	Maxwell
Magdalene	Marian	May
Maguire	Marianna	Maynard
Mahanoy City	Marietta	Maysville

311

Mayville	Menominee	Minden
Maywood	Mercedes	Mineola
McAdoo	Mercy	Minersville
McCabe	Meriden	Minerva
McCann	Merrill	Mingo Junction
McCarthy	Mesa	Minneapolis
McCauley	Methuen	Minnesota
McComb	Metuchen	Minnie
McCook	Mexico	Minot
McCormack	Meyer	Miranda
McDonald	Miami	Miriam
McGregor	Micah	Mission
McIntosh	Michael	Mississippi
McKee	Michigan	Missoula
McKeesport	Middleboro	Missouri
McKees Rocks	Middletown	Mitchell
McKenzie	Midland	Moberly
McKinney	Milan	Mobile
McLean	Mildred	Modesto
McLeod	Miles	Moira
McMillan	Miles City	Moline
McPherson	Milford	Monaca
Meadville	Milicent	Monessen
Mechanicsburg	Millburn	Monica
Mechanicville	Millbury	Monmouth
Medford	Milledgeville	Monroe
Melbourne	Miller	Monrovia
Melissa	Millvale	Montague
Melrose	Millville	Montana
Memphis	Milton	Montclair
Menasha	Milwaukee	Montebello

312

Monterey	Munich	Nathan
Montevideo	Murdock	Nathaniel
Montgomery	Murfreesboro	Natick
Montpelier	Muriel	Naugatuck
Montreal	Murphy	Nazareth
Moore	Murphysboro	Neal
Mooresville	Murray	Nebraska
Moorhead	Muscatine	Needham
Morgan	Muskegon	Neenah
Morgantown	Myers	Negaunee
Morocco	Myra	Nehemiah
Morris	Myrtle	Nellie
Morrison	Naaman	Nelson
Morristown	Nampa	Nelsonville
Morrisville	Nancy	Neptune
Morse	Nanking	Nerissa
Mortimer	Nannette	Netherlands
Moscow	Nanticoke	Nevada
Moses	Nanty-Glo	New Albany
Moultrie	Naomi	Newark
Moundsville	Napa	New Bedford
Mount Airy	Naperville	New Bern
Mount Carmel	Naples	Newberry
Mount Clemens	Napoleon	New Boston
Mount Kisco	Nash	New Braunfels
Mount Lebanon	Nashua	New Brighton
Mount Oliver	Nashville	New Britain
Mount Pleasant	Natal	New Brunswick
Mount Vernon	Natalie	Newburgh
Muncie	Natchez	Newburyport
Munhall	Natchitoches	New Castle

313

Newfoundland	North Adams	Oelwein
New Hampshire	Northampton	Ogden
New Haven	North Bergen	Ogdensburg
New Jersey	North Brad-dock	Ohio
New Kensington	Northbridge	Oil City
New London	North Carolina	Oklahoma
New Mexico	North Chicago	Oklahoma City
New Orleans	North Dakota	Okmulgee
Newport	North Platte	Old Forge
Newport News	Norwalk	Old Town
New Rochelle	Norway	Olean
Newton	Norwich	Olga
New Ulm	Norwood	Olive
New York	Nottingham	Oliver
New Zealand	Nova Scotia	Olney
Niagara Falls	Nuremberg	Olsen
Nicaragua	Nutley	Olson
Nicholas	Nyack	Olympia
Niles	Oakland	Olyphant
Niles Center	Oakmont	Omaha
Nina	Oak Park	Oneida
Noah	Oakwood	O'Neil
Noel	Obadiah	Oneonta
Nogales	O'Brien	Ontario
Nolan	Ocala	Opelika
Nora	O'Connor	Opelousas
Norfolk	Oconto	Ophelia
Norma	Octavia	Orange
Normal	Octavius	Orangeburg
Norman	Odessa	Oregon
Norristown	O'Donnell	Orlando

314

Oscar

Oshkosh

Oskaloosa

Oslo

Osmund

Ossining

Oswald

Oswego

Ottawa

Otto

Ottumwa

Owego

Owen

Owensboro

Owosso

Oxnard

Packard

Paducah

Painesville

Palestine

Palmer

Palmerton

Palmyra

Palo Alto

Pamela

Pampa

Panama

Pansy

Paraguay

Paris

Parker

Parkersburg

Park Ridge

Parma

Parsons

Pasadena

Pascagoula

Passaic

Patchogue

Paterson

Patience

Patricia

Patrick

Paul

Paula

Paulina

Pauline

Paulsboro

Pawtucket

Peabody

Peale

Pearl

Pearson

Peekskill

Peggy

Pekin

Pelham

Pendleton

Penns Grove

Pennsylvania

Penn Yan

Pensacola

Peoria

Percival

Percy

Perry

Perth Amboy

Peru

Petaluma

Peter

Petersburg

Petersen

Peterson

Petoskey

Phelps

Philadelphia

Philander

Philip

Philippa

Philippine Islands

Phillips

Phillipsburg

Phineas

Phoebe

Phoenix

Phoenixville

Phyllis

Piedmont

Pierce

Pine Bluff

Pitcairn

Pitman

Pittsburgh

315

Pittsfield	Pottsville	Ralph
Pittston	Poughkeepsie	Ramona
Pius	Powell	Randall
Plainfield	Powers	Randolph
Plains	Prague	Rankin
Plainview	Pratt	Rapid City
Plant City	Prescott	Raton
Plaquemine	Presque Isle	Ravenna
Plattsburg	Price	Ray
Pleasantville	Prichard	Raymond
Plymouth	Princeton	Reading
Pocatello	Priscilla	Reba
Poland	Providence	Rebecca
Polly	Provo	Red Bank
Ponca City	Prudence	Redlands
Pontiac	Pueblo	Red Oak
Portage	Puerto Rico	Red Wing
Portales	Pulaski	Redwood City
Port Angeles	Putnam	Regina
Port Arthur	Puyallup	Reginald
Port Chester	Quakertown	Reid
Porter	Quebec	Reidsville
Porterville	Queensland	Reinhardt
Port Huron	Quincy	Reno
Portia	Quinn	Renshaw
Port Jervis	Quito	Rensselaer
Portland	Rachel	Reuben
Portsmouth	Racine	Revere
Portugal	Radford	Rex
Potter	Rahway	Reynolds
Pottstown	Raleigh	Rhea

316

Rhinelander	Rocky Mount	Russia
Rhoda	Roderick	Ruston
Rhode Island	Roger	Ruth
Rhodes	Roland	Rutherford
Richard	Rolla	Rutland
Richfield	Rollo	Ryan
Richman	Romania	Rye
Richmond	Rome	Ryerson
Richwood	Romola	Saco
Ridgefield	Roosevelt	Sacramento
Ridgeway	Rosa	Saginaw
Ridgewood	Rosalind	Saguenay
Riga	Roscoe	St. Albans
Riley	Roselle	St. Augustine
Rio de Janeiro	Rosemary	St. Bernard
Rita	Roseville	St. Charles
River Rouge	Ross	St. Clair
Riverside	Rossville	St. Cloud
Roanoke	Roswell	St. John
Robbins	Rotterdam	St. Johnsbury
Robbinsdale	Rowena	St. Joseph
Robert	Roy	St. Louis
Robertson	Royal Oak	St. Marys
Robinson	Ruby	St. Paul
Robstown	Rudolph	St. Peter
Rochester	Rufus	St. Petersburg
Rockford	Rumford Falls	Salamanca
Rock Island	Rupert	Salem
Rockland	Rushville	Salina
Rock Springs	Rusk	Salinas
Rockville	Russell	Salisbury

317

Salome	Santa Monica	Seattle
Salt Lake City	Santa Paula	Secaucus
Sampson	Santa Rosa	Sedalia
Samuel	Santiago	Selma
San Angelo	Sapulpa	Seminole
San Anselmo	Sarah	Seneca Falls
San Antonio	Saranac Lake	Serena
San Benito	Sarasota	Seth
San Bernardino	Saratoga Springs	Seville
San Bruno	Saugus	Seward
Sanders	Saul	Sewickley
San Diego	Sault Ste. Marie	Sexton
Sand Springs	Saunders	Seymour
Sandusky	Savannah	Shaker Heights
San Fernando	Sawyer	Shamokin
Sanford	Sayre	Shanghai
San Francisco	Sayreville	Sharon
San Gabriel	Scarsdale	Sharp
San Jose	Schenectady	Sharpsburg
San Leandro	Schmidt	Sharpsville
San Luis Obispo	Schneider	Shaw
San Marcos	Schroeder	Shawnee
San Marino	Schultz	Shea
San Mateo	Schuyler	Sheboygan
San Rafael	Schwartz	Sheffield
Santa Ana	Scotia	Sheila
Santa Barbara	Scotland	Shelby
Santa Clara	Scott	Shelbyville
Santa Cruz	Scottdale	Sheldon
Santa Fe	Scottsbluff	Shenandoah
Santa Maria	Scranton	Sheridan

318

Sherman	Somerset	Stalingrad
Sherwood	Somerville	Stamford
Shippensburg	Somersworth	Stanford
Shirley	Sonora	Stanley
Shoemaker	Sophia	State College
Shorewood	Sophronia	Statesboro
Shreveport	Sorensen	Statesville
Siam	South Africa	Staunton
Sibyl	South Amboy	Steelton
Sicily	South America	Stella
Sidney	South Bend	Stephen
Siegal	South Boston	Sterling
Siegfried	Southbridge	Steubenville
Sikeston	South Carolina	Stevens
Silas	South Dakota	Stewart
Silvanus	South Hadley	Stillwater
Silvester	Southampton	Stockholm
Silvia	Southington	Stockton
Simmons	South Orange	Stone
Simon	South River	Stoneham
Simpson	Spain	Storm Lake
Sinclair	Sparks	Stoughton
Singapore	Sparta	Stowe
Sioux City	Spartanburg	Stratford
Sioux Falls	Spencer	Straus
Skinner	Spokane	Streator
Sloan	Sprague	Stroudsburg
Smith	Springfield	Struthers
Snyder	Spring Valley	Stuart
Soloman	Stacey	Sturgeon Bay
Solvay	Stafford	Sturgis

Stuttgart	Tampa	Tifton
Sudan	Tampico	Tilda
Suffolk	Tarboro	Timothy
Sullivan	Tarentum	Tipton
Summit	Tarrytown	Titus
Sumner	Tasmania	Titusville
Sumter	Taunton	Tobiah
Sunbury	Taylor	Tokyo
Superior	Taylorville	Toledo
Susan	Teaneck	Tonawanda
Swampscott	Temple	Tony
Swansea	Tenafly	Toole
Sweden	Tennessee	Topeka
Sweetwater	Terence	Toronto
Swift	Terre Haute	Torrance
Swissvale	Terrel	Torrington
Switzerland	Terry	Toulouse
Sybil	Texarkana	Trenton
Sydney	Texas	Trieste
Sylvanus	Texas City	Trinidad
Sylvester	Thaddeus	Tripoli
Sylvia	Thalia	Troy
Syracuse	Thea	Truman
Syria	The Hague	Tuckahoe
Tabitha	Theodore	Tucson
Tacoma	Theodora	Tulane
Taft	Theresa	Tulsa
Talladega	Thomas	Tunis
Tallahassee	Thomaston	Tupelo
Tallulah	Thomasville	Turin
Tamaqua	Tiffin	Turkey

320

Turner	Vance	Waddington
Tuscaloosa	Vanderlip	Wadsworth
Tuscumbia	Van Dyke	Wakefield
Twin Falls	Van Horn	Wales
Tyler	Van Wert	Walker
Tyrone	Vatican City	Wallace
Ukraine	Vaughan	Walla Walla
Ulrich	Venezuela	Wallingford
Ulysses	Venice	Wallington
Underhill	Ventnor City	Walpole
Underwood	Vera Cruz	Walsenburg
Union	Vermont	Walsh
Union City	Vernon	Walter
United Kingdom	Verona	Waltham
United States	Veronica	Ward
Upland	Vicksburg	Ware
Upton	Victor	Warren
Urban	Victoria	Warrensburg
Urbana	Villa Park	Warsaw
Uriah	Vincennes	Warwick
Ursula	Vincent	Washington
Uruguay	Vineland	Waterbury
Utah	Vienna	Waterloo
Utica	Viola	Watertown
Vail	Violet	Waterville
Valdosta	Virgil	Watervliet
Valentine	Virginia	Watson
Valeria	Visalia	Watsonville
Valley City	Vivian	Waukegan
Valley Stream	Wabash	Waukesha
Valparaiso	Waco	Waupun

Wausau

Waverly

Waxahachie

Waycross

Waynesboro

Weatherford

Webb City

Webster

Welch

Wellesley

Wellington

Wellsburg

Wellston

Wellsville

Wenatchee

Wesley

West Allis

West Bend

Westbrook

West Chester

Westerly

Westfield

West Haven

West New York

Weston

West Orange

West Point

West View

West Virginia

Westwood

West York

Weymouth

Wheaton

Wheeling

White

White Plains

Whiting

Whitman

Whittier

Wichita

Wilbur

Wildwood

Wilfred

Wilkes-Barre

Wilkinsburg

Willard

William

Williamson

Williamsport

Willimantic

Williston

Willmar

Wilmerding

Wilmette

Wilmington

Wilson

Winchester

Windber

Winfield

Winifred

Winnetka

Winnipeg

Winona

Winooski

Winslow

Winsted

Winston-Salem

Winter

Winthrop

Winton

Wisconsin

Woburn

Wolf

Wood

Woodbridge

Woodbury

Woodland

Wood River

Woodruff

Woodstock

Woodward

Woonsocket

Wooster

Worcester

Worthington

Wyandotte

Wyoming

Xenia

Yakima

Yankton

Yates

Yazoo City

Yokohama

322

Yonkers	Ypsilanti	Yvonne
York	Yucatan	Zanesville
Young	Yugoslavia	Zenobia
Youngstown	Yuma	Zion

PART THREE
ABBREVIATIONS

Some expressions are dictated and transcribed almost exclusively in abbreviated form, such as *f.o.b.* Some expressions may be dictated and transcribed either in full or in the form of initials, such as *A.C.* or *alternating current*. The following list contains 72 such expressions with a legible shorthand outline for each set of initials.

AAF	Army Air Forces	
ABC	American Broadcasting Company	
A.C.	alternating current	
A.D.	*anno Domini*	
AEC	Atomic Energy Commission	
A.F. of L.	American Federation of Labor	
A.L.P.	American Labor Party	
a.m.	ante meridiem	
A.M.A.	American Medical Association	
A.O.L.	absent over leave	
APO	Army Post Office	
A.S.C.A.P.	American Society of Composers, Authors, and Publishers	
ASTP	Army Specialized Training Program	

A.W.O.L.	absent without leave	
B.B.A.	Bachelor of Business Administration	
B.B.C.	British Broadcasting Corporation	
B.I.S.	Bank for International Settlements	
BLS	Bureau of Labor Statistics	
B.t.u.	British thermal unit	
CBI	China, Burma, India	
CBS	Columbia Broadcasting System	
cc.	cubic centimeters	
c.i.f.	cost, insurance, and freight	
C.I.O.	Congress of Industrial Organizations	
C.O.D.	collect on delivery	
C.P.A.	Certified Public Accountant	
C.S.R.	Certified Shorthand Reporter	
c.w.o.	cash with order	
D.A.	District Attorney	
D.A.R.	Daughters of the American Revolution	
D.C.	direct current	
D.D.S.	Doctor of Dental Surgery	
DP	displaced person	

DX	distance	
E. & O.E.	errors and omissions excepted	
Ed. D.	Doctor of Education	
E.Q.	educational quotient	
ERP	European Recovery Program	
ETO	European Theater of Operation	
FCC	Federal Communications Commission	
FDIC	Federal Deposit Insurance Corporation	
FM	frequency modulation	
f.o.b.	free on board	
FPC	Federal Power Commission	
FSA	Federal Security Agency	
FTC	Federal Trade Commission	
GHQ	General Headquarters	
HOLC	Home Owners Loan Corporation	
ICC	Interstate Commerce Commission	
I.L.O.	International Labor Organization	
IQ	intelligence quotient	
ITO	International Trade Organization	
M.D.	Doctor of Medicine	

NBC	National Broadcasting Company
N.E.A.	National Education Association
NLRB	National Labor Relations Board
OPA	Office of Price Administration
OSS	Office of Strategic Services
PBX	private branch exchange
p.m.	post meridiem
P.S.	postscript
P.T.A.	Parent-Teacher Association
q.v.	which see
R.F.D.	Rural Free Delivery
ROTC	Reserve Officers' Training Corps
r.p.m.	revolutions per minute
TNT	trinitrotoluene
TVA	Tennessee Valley Authority
USES	United States Employment Service
VA	Veterans' Administration
W.F.T.U.	World Federation of Trade Unions
WPA	Works Progress Administration